FAITH, HOPE AND MALTA GC

FAITH, HOPE AND MALTA GC

Ground and Air Heroes of the George Cross Island

Tony Spooner
DSO, DFC

A Goodall paperback
from
Crécy Publishing Limited

First published in Great Britain by
Newton Publishers 1992
This edition published by
Crécy Publishing Limited, 2008

ISBN 9 780907 579588

Front cover photograph courtesy of the Imperial War Museum (A13425)
Back cover courtesy Jim Pickering

Printed by Progress Press, Malta

A Goodall paperback
published by

Crécy Publishing Limited
1a Ringway Trading Estate, Shadowmoss Road, Manchester M22 5LH

To the 2,301 airmen of the Commonwealth whose names appear in the Air Force's Memorial in Valletta, Malta. They fell in raids or on sorties during WW II and have no known grave other than the water of the Mediterranean.

CONTENTS

ACKNOWLEDGEMENTS

It is not sufficient to acknowledge, with thanks, the generous contributions made to this book by the many airmen and aircrew whose names, photographs and accounts appear within. My thanks must also go to the 41 other Air Force contributors who also sent me similar research material.

It also helped to create in my mind a better picture of what it was like to have been on Malta between 1940–1943. The explanation of why such valuable contributions had to be omitted is that, in all, I received about a quarter of a million words which described what those who were there at this critical time in history, had to endure. With the island isolated and besieged, it was plenty. To reduce 250,000 words to a more acceptable 75,000 words, or so, required drastic surgery.

I must even apologise to the dozen or so contributors whose accounts do appear, as in their cases their accounts too had to be much reduced. Ken Rogers, for example, sent me over 30,000 words and I would have liked to have included them all. The diaries of Mary Bates, Len Williamson, Bill Metcalf, etc, were also well worth producing at greater length.

A special thanks must go to Richard Slater who, as well as personally contributing, also 'spread the gospel' to others and thereby added to my wealth of material. John Alton went one better, he sent me a dozen or so excellent stories which he had collected from others who were there. Len Williamson's superb diaries would not have reached me but for Ivor Broom and, likewise, it was Gordon Excell who led me to Bill Metcalf's very humane ones.

I am especially in debt to Norman Franks, author and historian, and a man with over 25 of his own wartime books published, who kindly edited and checked the entire work and who added confirmatory snippets of information from his own considerable knowledge and research. Norman played a major part in reducing this book to an acceptable length. In a sense, it is as much his book as mine.

Finally I wish to thank both Ivor Broom and my wife Anne, for carefully reading the work and for eliminating the many small but annoying spelling and grammatical mistakes to which I am all too prone.

TONY SPOONER

N

GOZO

0 1 2 3 Miles
0 1 2 3 4 5 Kilometres

Comino

St. Paul's Bay

Mosta   Naxxar

Intarfa Hospital   Takali
Rabat

MALTA

Luqa
Krendi   Kirkup
Safi

Fifla   Hal Far

Kalafrana

FOREWORD

Air Marshal Sir Ivor Broom KCB, CBE, DSO, DFC, AFC

This is the most comprehensive book I have read about the Air Forces at Malta during World War 11. Much has been written, quite rightly, about the heroic defence of the island by the few fighter squadrons and anti-aircraft batteries and about the Royal Navy's courage and determination to re-supply the island with essential war material and basic food rations – and this book adds to those epic stories about Malta under seige.

It is also, however, a book which shows Malta on the offensive and which highlights the key role Malta played in the ultimate allied victory in Europe. The chapter headings give some indication of the wide ranging offensive operations by many types of aircraft – bombers, reconnaissance, torpedo and 'special duties'. Malta truly was the 'unsinkable aircraft carrier' and despite incessant bombing, particularly from late 1941 to mid 1942, it remained a springboard for attack against shipping carrying supplies to Rommel in North Africa. The author provides the mind-boggling statistic that in April 1942, more bombs were dropped on this small island, (smaller than the Isle of Wight) than on the whole of the British Isles in any month during the Battle of Britain – but still the Malta squadrons continued their attacks on enemy targets.

Aircraft and aircrew losses were particularly heavy so, operational aircrew, generally speaking, and with a few notable exceptions such as Warburton, did relatively short tours of duty in Malta. On the other hand, the ground staff and local population suffered much hardship for many years. It is very humbling for me, as a pilot who operated from Malta for four months, to be reminded of the endurance of those on the ground.

Adversity brings out the best in people and nowhere was this shown better than amongst those at Malta who provided the many different supporting services which the aircrew need to operate effectively. Day after day, on meagre and monotonous rations, and under incessant air attack, they stuck to their tasks with great determination and good humour. Chapter Seven, which comes from Ken Rogers' 'diary', typifies the spirit of the time. He makes light of the very real hardships, and jokes about the rations – small wonder that Malta survived with ground staff such as he to support the aircrew.

The reconnaissance aircraft, the bomber/torpedo aircraft and the air defence fighters, provided what the author describes as 'the eyes, the punch, the guard.' All three aspects, plus the men and women of the supporting services, provide the theme of this fascinating book.

INTRODUCTION

To get a true picture of what it was like to be serving the RAF during the heat of war, it is generally necessary to study the viewpoints of the airmen who serviced the planes as well as those of the men who flew in them. Nowhere is this more necessary than when recounting the war in the air in, and around, Malta 1940–1942.

There, during those years, the aircraft on the ground and those who patched up and serviced them became the direct targets of everything that the Luftwaffe and Regia Aeronautica could, and continually did, throw at them, often at point-blank range, too. This is why this book has a sandwich-like construction: after an account or two of what took place in the air, there follows an account or two of what it was like to be on the ground at the time.

The interplay between airmen and aircrew is deliberate. Without the great efforts of those who worked around the clock on the ground under simply appalling conditions – a surfeit of bombs, a shortage of all else, there could have been no aircraft to defend the island fortress nor to mount any offensive strike from Malta. Each was dependent upon the other for survival.

Moreover, as the Epilogue shows, the effect made upon the overall pattern of the war by this unshakeable combination of men in Air Force blue, was out of all proportion to the tiny size of the island and to the relatively small number of planes and men involved.

Many a post war study has concluded that Malta was the key to Allied victory in Europe. Who am I to disagree? I was there.

Few, if any, have expressed Malta's defiance better than the American President, Franklin D Roosevelt, who presented the island with an illuminated scroll, which reads:

> In the name of the people of the United States of America, I salute the island of Malta, it's people and defenders, who in the cause of freedom and justice and decency throughout the world, have rendered valorous service far above and beyond the call of duty.
>
> Under repeated fire from the skies, Malta stood alone but unafraid in the center of the sea, one tiny bright flame in the

darkness... a beacon of hope for the clearer days which have come.

Malta's bright story of human fortitude and courage will be read by posterity with wonder and with gratitude through all the ages. What was done in this Island maintains the highest traditions of gallant men and women who from the beginning of time have lived and died to preserve civilization for all mankind.'

PREFACE

The public address system broke the silence in the plane... 'In a few minutes time we shall be landing at Luqa airport, Malta... please fasten your seat-belts...' The young honeymoon couple smiled at each other. They had made it. Soon they would be at the hotel.

She felt a slight blush rising and looked out of the window just as the jet banked around. The whole island came into focus. 'How small it is,' she mused, 'small but lovely with the evening sun casting shadows on the pale limestone which contrasts with the deep blue all around.' She was glad that her Roger had chosen this famous holiday island for their honeymoon.

'How peaceful it looks,' she said half aloud. Her husband caught the words. 'It wasn't always like this,' he informed her, 'It went through such Hell during the last big war that the King gave it a GC.' She looked puzzled:

'A GC, what's that?'

'It stands for George Cross. It's a very rare medal: even more rare than the Victoria Cross.'

'But surely, they give medals to people, not places?'

'You're right,' he agreed, 'but this was an exception: the only one ever made. You see,... as I said, the island went through such Hell that King George wanted to make it very special. Some people when they write letters even put 'Malta GC' on the envelope.'

'You know a lot about it,' she said, 'Did they teach you this at the Tech?'

'No. Dad likes to talk about it at home. He wasn't here; it all happened about 50 years ago. Dad had an uncle here and that got him interested. The uncle got shot-up too and died quite soon after the war.'

'Was he flying one of those Spitfires, or whatever it is that those old planes were called?'

'No, he was one of the chaps who looked after them on the ground.'

'But,' she questioned, 'I thought that is was only pilots who got shot-up?' He smiled: 'Wrong again. Malta was different. They had to put up with over three thousand air raids: far more than even London got and you can see how small this place is. Almost everyone in Malta got bombed.'

He paused as the wheels thumped down, but continued: 'I suppose that hearing Dad talk about it gave me the idea of us coming here now. I've always wanted to see the places which I've read about in the books that Dad bought. I believe that the RAF, and everyone else here, just about ran out of food too.'

He paused again, wondering whether to go on but she merely squeezed his hand. She was happy to hear him ramble on and, anyhow, they would be out in the sunshine soon. 'The island was then British,' he continued, 'and had been so ever since Nelson was here…' As the jet came to a halt in front of the terminal building, she caught the words, 'Until the 10th of June, 1940, the island of Malta, nestling quietly in the middle of the Mediterranean, had not had an unpleasant war…'

CHAPTER ONE

FAITH, HOPE – AND HURRICANES

Until 10 June, 1940, the island of Malta, nestling quietly in the Mediterranean, had had a quiet and not unpleasant war. It was only on that day that the Italian Dictator, Benito Mussolini, brought his country into the war on the side of her so far victorious German ally and so began Malta's travail from the new Axis forces.

The fall of Paris just four days later, followed by the total French collapse by the 17th, further added to Malta's plight. Pre-war, the Anglo-French understanding was that the huge French fleet would, in the event of war between that alliance and Italy, take care of the equally modern and impressive – at least on paper – Italian fleet. Now, with the surrender of France, the balance of naval power in the Mediterranean altered dramatically. With many responsibilities elsewhere, only a small portion of the large British fleet could be spared to take care of the Italian threat.

Malta was so unprepared for war, especially a war without French support, that the British War Cabinet all but decided to abandon the island to Mussolini. Fortunately, with the change of Prime Minister, the War Cabinet had voted on 28 May, by just 3 to 2, not to offer Malta together with other British and French territories to Mussolini in the hope that such a gesture would keep Italy out of the war. The Coalition War Cabinet's two Conservatives, Chamberlain and Lord Halifax voted for the surrender, while Churchill and the two Socialists, Attlee and Greenwood, won the vote.

Soon after dawn on day two of Italy's war, she bombed Malta; the island having no 'official' air defence and very few anti aircraft guns. But it did have some 'unofficial fighter defence'. Strangely enough it had been the sinking of the British aircraft carrier *HMS Glorious* during the Narvik campaign in April 1940, that led to the island having any fighter aircraft at all at this time. Prior to the declaration of war by Italy, there was, sitting in the Navy yard at Kalafrana, a number of boxed Sea Gladiator biplane fighters, crated up ready to be transferred to the *Glorious* when required. That requirement had now been taken away.

There followed a number of almost farcical orders and counter orders. The aircraft were seized by some enterprising RAF individuals and hastily put together, only to be put back into crates, by the Navy no doubt, when this was discovered. However, the RAF, led by some far seeing, brilliant engineers, notably Squadron Leader A E Louks, persisted and, with the backing of the AOC – Air Commodore F H M 'Sammy' Maynard, himself a First War Naval fighter pilot – won the day. Louks, who was also a pilot, even test flew the reassembled biplanes. In total there were fifteen Gladiators but three were eventually sent to the Middle East, while four more went aboard *HMS Eagle*. This left just eight and some of these had to be cannabalised for spares.

Initially four Gladiators were ready and prepared by 10 June – and became the Malta Fighter Flight. But aircraft were one thing, pilots another. There were no experienced fighter pilots available on the island, either RAF or Fleet Air Arm, so pilots of any kind were recruited. There was an RAF Admin. HQ on the island and from this four or five pilots, all of whom volunteered, emerged. The rest is history.

One pilot, who was later put in charge of this small, unique band, was Flight Lieutenant (later Squadron Leader) George Burges, a very fit and hearty man, who until now had been a flying boat captain. On the first day, he led three Gladiators to intercept three waves of SM79 tri-motored bombers (a total of 55) escorted by 18 MC200 fighters. Burges put some holes in one Savoia, and Flying Officer W J 'Timber' Woods forced a Macchi fighter down and away, but that was the sole damage inflicted, although not bad for three against 73! However, this first skirmish was merely the start of nearly two and a half years of desperate fighting in defence of the island.

* * *

The Gladiators did not shoot down any great numbers of enemy aircraft which is not surprising since the Italians went to war with fast and efficient aeroplanes for the period. Their principal bomber was the Savoia-Machetti 79, while fighters consisted of a high performance and extremely manoeuvrable biplane, the Fiat CR42, and a fast modern monoplane, the Macchi 200, soon to be supplemented by the Mc 202. However, the Gladiators put up such a sterling resistance that the Italians, who thought the island had no air defence, had to reshape their pre-conceived ideas about swiftly dominating Malta and bombing its people into early submission.

The bombers now began to fly over with huge fighter escort. Under George Burges' inspired leadership and with help from Arthur Edward Louks, who modified the Gladiators so as to give them a better rate of climb, the RAF not only made the Italians think again, they also won the applause and acclaim of the Maltese people, who, for the remainder of the war, were quite definitely on the British side and vehemently anti-Italian; later equally anti-German. The value of both these results of the gallant fight against odds put up by George Burges and his colleagues was without price.

George shot down the first Italian, a single SM79 on a recce mission on 22 June. He was also the first of many Malta based pilots to receive the Distinguished Flying Cross. A Gladiator was the first Malta aircraft to be shot down and later, Flight Lieutenant P G Keeble became the first RAF pilot to be shot down and killed over the island. In his case he brought down an enemy aircraft with him – both crashing within yards of each other.

All this showed the British Government that Malta could indeed be defended and steps were taken to send out trained fighter pilots in more modern aircraft to the island, although following the Battle of France and with the Battle of Britain about to begin, it was not the best time to take either from Fighter Command's already depleted force.

However, the Italian Air Force (Regia Aeronautica) was shown up to be far less effective than had been thought, which had repercussions that spread to the Middle East and beyond. The life and death struggle being seen displayed over Malta in those early days was a real morale booster to a Britain seemingly surrounded by one disaster after another.

When asked about the famous names given to the Gladiators, George Burges is quite adamant that in his day – and he was to remain on the island for almost another year – the three biplanes were never called 'Faith, Hope and Charity'. For one thing there were four initially and after some had been destroyed or damaged, another two were assembled. There was also a hybrid plane constructed from a damaged Gladiator and parts from a crashed Swordfish and a Blenheim! It never went into action but is thought to have been test flown by Louks or another engineer, before it was destroyed by a bomb. One Gladiator at least, survived many years and there is a record of it being used on Met. flights and possibly on Air Sea Rescue searches as late as 1942. However, by the end of June 1940, they had really had their day and served their purpose, when the first Hurricanes began to arrive.

* * *

The first Hurricane fighters to arrive on Malta landed on 21 June – just two from an original batch of six destined originally for Alexandria. Six more arrived from England via France the next day, although three were soon sent off to Alexandria, leaving just five with the island defenders. As July began, the Hurricanes stood ready with the remining Gladiators to do battle; the Hurricanes shooting down their first Italian on the 3rd. It was another SM79, shot down by Flying Officer John Waters who in turn was shot down by a CR42 escort – whose pilot thought he'd shot down a Spitfire!

Once France fell, Hurricanes could no longer be flown to Malta in stages from England, so the Navy put their ancient carrier *HMS Argus* at the RAF's disposal in order to take fighters through the Mediterranean. Twelve Hurricanes were put aboard her and she sailed from the Clyde, heading for Gibraltar, then through the Straits sailing east. When 350–400 miles west of Malta, the Hurricanes, led by two Fleet Air Arm Skua aircraft, successfully took off from the carrier and all landed safely on the island. The date was 2 August, 1940 – yet another date to be added to those on which events occurred which helped save Malta. In the event, it was to be this mode of transport which was to dominate the reinforcement of the island with fighter aircraft.

However, this method was nearly scotched when a second attempt was made on 17 November. On this occasion, the Hurricanes were sent off when still too far from the island because of reports of enemy ships. A strong head wind didn't help either. Of the 12 fighters, only four reached the island – just, while all the others fell into the sea with empty fuel tanks. It would not be until 3 April, 1941 that another carrier attempt would be made. Nevertheless, by November 1941, no fewer than 333 Hurricanes had been delivered to the island by carrier flights. Only 28 had failed to make it, including the eight on 17 November 1940. The

other carriers which made these gallant runs were *HMS Ark Royal,
Furious* and *Victorious*. However, of the 333, about 150 were
subsequently flown on to the Middle East.

Despite these numbers, there was rarely more than a handful
available to defend the island, but the pilots did so valiantly, against
fantastic odds. When the Italians turned to night bombing, the
Hurricane pilots even turned their hand to night fighting, the pilots
often being guided to the enemy by the use of searchlights.

By the end of 1940, the Malta Fighter Flight had become No 261
Squadron. Its pilots could acccount for the majority of the 35
hostile aircraft the Italians were prepared to admit they had lost,
along with many more damaged. The average strength of the
Squadron appears to have been about 18 Hurricanes plus three or
four Gladiators. On the few occasions the army in North Africa
managed to push the Germans and Italians to the west, some
Hurricanes were flown across to Malta from Derna or Benghazi,
but they were rare occasions.

The happy situation of a few Hurricanes having the upper hand
over large numbers of the Regia Aeronautica was not to last. Firstly
the enemy introduced the much dreaded Ju 87 'Stuka' dive-bomber
into the struggle. This machine had caused havoc in France
although it had been defeated over England. Against shipping and
airfields on Malta it was again a deadly accurate machine. Its initial
impact into the Malta battle was small because it was flown by
Italian pilots. Soon thereafter, a far more purposeful enemy took a
hand. The Luftwaffe arrived in Sicily in force.

* * *

The arrival of the German Luftwaffe over Malta at the beginning of
1941, showed that the enemy meant business and soon rumours of
a possible invasion were rife. With the Italians failing in their battles
in North Africa and Greece, Hitler had to step in to bolster his Axis
partner and Malta, now more than ever, needed to be neutralised in
order to safeguard Axis shipping routes across the Mediterranean.

The German pilots were an experienced lot, having seen action
over France and England. Their Me 109F fighters were far superior
to the Italian Fiats and Macchis and much more of a match for the
poor Hurricanes of 261 Squadron. The revised situation came to be

sharply realised when the giant, modern, carrier *HMS Illustrious* came under fire. She was hit several times by dive bombers, both Ju 87s and Ju 88s, while escorting a convoy to Malta from the Eastern Mediterranean. Listing badly and with 126 dead seamen and 91 wounded on board, she limped into Malta for desperately needed repairs on 10 January. There followed what has become known as the 'Illustrious Blitz'.

The carrier was hidden in French Creek but within days the Germans had spotted her. Bombs rained down as never before; many of them deadly accurate, delivered by almost recklessly brave German pilots. Not only was the harbour of Valletta blitzed to such an extent that the city surrounding it was virtually reduced to rubble and abandoned, but the nearby airfields from which the fighters rose to engage them, were likewise subjected to massive attacks. Every hangar, every building, was flattened. Craters dotted the runways and were bravely filled in almost as fast as they were made. Malta was never the same again. Air losses on both sides were considerable.

The defenders saved *HMS Illustrious* and she limped out of Grand Harbour on the 23rd, heading for Alexandria. But the cost to the defenders was grave. There was hardly a serviceable Hurricane or Gladiator left at Ta Kali. Even FAA Fulmers, with even poorer performance than the Hurricanes, had joined in the air battles. They had come from the battered carrier and one pilot at least, made a name for himself in this fight. Lieutenant Jackie Sewell (a great friend and flying collegue of the author, pre-war), was credited with 9 enemy planes shot down, many during those hectic few days. The Fulmars operated from Hal Far, which was also almost rubbed off the map during the Illustrious Blitz.

The Luftwaffe continued to menace the island during the early spring of 1941. The Hurricanes found it difficult even to catch the fairly fast Ju 88 bomber and dive-bomber. The Ju 87s were easy to catch immediately after their near vertical dive but by then they could have inflicted vital damage. The 109s were always a problem. One of the leading Messerschmitt pilots was Joachim Muncheberg, who led the 7th Staffel of JG26. He and his men seemed invulnerable for they claimed any number of Hurricanes shot down without losing one of their own fighters.

Replacement RAF pilots and Hurricanes made good the continued losses, some pilots coming in by Sunderland flying boat or Wellington bomber after dark. Perhaps the worst day for 261 Squadron was 22 March. They managed to get eight machines into the air only to have five shot down without loss to the Luftwaffe. It was an unequal struggle. Both pilots and planes were tired but unlike pilots in England, there was little time for rest on Malta. Lack of spares for the Hurricanes made things even worse.

After Greece and Yugoslavia had been overrun and Crete had fallen, Malta became still further isolated. Newer and slightly more modern Hurricanes did arrive, both by carrier or occasionally by merchant ship but few lasted long.

However, there was just enough to form a second fighter squadron, and No 185 was born at Hal Far on 12 May. New names began to emerge. Flight Lieutenant J A F MacLachlan DFC, a young part-New Zealander who had seen action during Battles in France, and Innes Westmacott DFC, who had fought in the Battle of Britain. In a period when morale was sinking due to sustained losses, they stood out and helped to inspire others. 'Mac', after being shot down and losing an arm, won a bet that within weeks he would be flying again. He won this by taking up the Station's small Magister and flying it one handed. Invalided back to the UK, he fought on with the aid of an artificial arm, becoming an even more successful intruder pilot, before meeting his end over Germany.

Innes Westmacott happily survived the war, but died in late 1991, just a few months before the 50th anniversary celebrations of the Malta Fight and Siege. Quite apart from his activities with 185 Squadron he also indulged in some clandestine visits to Sicily which involved dropping money to an agent who was half way up Mount Etna – at night! He also flew some night fighting missions.

The Malta Night Fighting Unit (MNFU) was another Malta invention and its spark-plug was another character. George Powell-Shedden DFC, commonly known as 'Polly' was a huge hulk of a man who spluttered and stuttered his way around Luqa. He and Donald 'Dimsie' Stones DFC (both men were Battle of Britain veterans) had flown out to take command of something, only to find nobody knew what or why. So Polly was put in charge of the MNFU, whose job it was to defend the island against night bombers. Later they also sought to seek out enemy aircraft over their home bases on Sicily. He, Dimsie, 'Cass' Cassidy, David Barnwell and Jackie Grant did splendid work with MNFU; for their

Hurricanes had no airborne radar or other means of finding the enemy in the dark. When not flying, Powell-Shedden could be found prowling around the airfield, helping to deal with unexploded bombs, the flare-path, or anything else which took his fancy. He was that kind of a man: impossible to ignore, although his stutter rendered him almost speechless at times.

Relief came for the island and the Hurricane pilots when the Germans, in preparation for their attack upon Russia in June, withdrew most of their aircraft from Sicily – including the dreaded 7/JG 26. Thus the summer of 1941 proved to be a relatively pleasant lull in the air fighting with newly arrived Hurricanes once again proving themselves capable of taking on the Italians.

June also saw the arrival of a new attack minded AOC – Hugh Pughe Lloyd, rapidly promoted from Group Captain to Air Vice Marshal. His orders were to stop supplies reaching Rommel and his Afrika Korps in North Africa, and it proved a well chosen appointment.

He arrived at a time when morale was rising, with more Hurricanes arriving too: and new units operating from Ta Kali –126 and 249 Squadrons.

One of the new fighter commanders was 'Ragbags' – Squadron Leader A C 'Sandy' Rabagliati. He quickly proved himself an able leader in the air and seldom missed an opportunity to aid Hugh Pughe (as everyone called the new AOC) in an offensive role. The Hurricanes were now shooting up Italian bombers on the ground on their bases in Sicily, the sun was shining, incoming raids decreased, successes mounted and losses decreased. But if anyone thought that the tide had turned, they were wrong.

* * *

With attacks on Malta having dwindled, RAF strength was increased. Luqa, with its longer runways, became the home of Blenheims and Wellingtons and the occasional Beaufort or Beaufighter. The Wellingtons were used for night bombing, the Blenheims for anti-shipping strikes. Hal Far, the FAA airfield, was the home of the successful Swordfish bombers of No 830 Squadron; later reinforced by the Albacores of 828 Squadron. Both were antique looking torpedo or bomb carrying biplanes, the former having open cockpits for it's two or three man crews.

Added to the island's striking force were submarines and the occasional surface ship, which were able to operate from this strategic base during this lull period. Enemy ships were now being sunk or damaged at an alarming rate; Rommel being denied war's lifeblood of fuel and ammunition. With the approach of winter, and with the German army in Russia temporarily halted, Rommel's cry for help to support a new desert offensive was answered by Luftwaffe units returning back to Sicily. Malta's plight began all over again.

By now, the island was running short of almost everything, from food and guns to fuel. It was essential to get supplies to it in such quantities that only ship convoys could provide. Up to a point, RAF Sunderlands had been bringing in spares and crew members but after Muncheberg had taken a fancy to destroying every Sunderland he ever saw on the water, even this supply method had been curtailed. By December 1941, Malta was again being blitzed as never before.

Hitler himself had refused Field Marshal Kesselring's (commander of Luftlotte II and now commander of all Axis forces in the area) request to invade the island – the heavy cost of capturing Crete still very much on his mind – but had agreed to sink it with bombs! Once again the Hurricanes, many now armed with cannon, proved a poor match for the more advanced models of Me 109, and once again the island had to suffer unmercifully.

The Big Blitz on Malta began in December. Both sides had come to realise fully the importance of Malta in the Middle East campaign. If Rommel was to succeed in his drive towards the oil fields of Arabia, he had to be supplied, and supplied regularly. Only Malta stood in the way.

Flying time from Sicily to Malta was just a few minutes and the targets easily identified. Maximum bomb loads could always be carried as fuel was minimal. Fresh from their victories and successes in Russia, the highly experienced Luftwaffe pilots threw themselves into the task of smashing Malta and its airfields. Against this the relatively few Hurricane Mark Is and Mark IIs were both outclassed and terribly outnumbered.

Few will forget that terrible winter. There was no fuel for heating. Food became scarcer and scarcer. The weather was vile – rain and chill predominated. Men went around in wet clothes after a night between damp blankets. Yet the exceptionally bad weather was almost a blessing as there were, mercifully, many days when the Luftwaffe couldn't operate.

The Hurricanes, most gallantly led by 'Ragbags' – now a Wing Commander – did their best both over Malta and over Sicily but could not stop the rain of bombs falling on the island. The Italians continued to attack also, bombing by day and night. With no modern night fighter aircraft, the air raid sirens wailing almost non-stop, the populace had to spend most of the 24 hours each day in their dark, damp and insanitary shelters. Health suffered. Skin diseases, polio, fevers, dysentery, bed bugs, lice, chills, etc, abounded. The lack of soap and disinfectant contributed.

The Hurricanes had had their day. Twice they had seen off the Italian Air Force. Now, it seemed, even the most uneducated peasant was saying: 'We want Spitfires!' The very word was assuming magic powers.

March 1942 seemed never ending. That month nearly 2,000 tons of bombs fell upon the harbour and the three main airfields. So short was ammunition for the anti-aircraft gunners that orders were issued that only bombers would be fired at – not fighters – and even then shells were rationed daily. To deal with low flying fighters, rifles were issued to gunners and ground personnel, not only to use in case of invasion, but to fire at the Messerschmitts when they strafed the airfields. Decoy aircraft were set up, some made of wood, many just aircraft long ago written off. Safi Strip, which resembled a runway from the air, soon became a graveyard for the dozens of written-off aeroplanes. They were lined up or propped up as best they could be. Again and again the enemy wasted bombs upon this useless collection.

Due to the intensity of the Blitz, the bombers and submarines were withdrawn. Yet if March was bad, April was far worse. That month the enemy dropped 6,728 tons of bombs, mainly on the airfields and harbour. This tonnage was greater than the monthly tonnage dropped against the whole of Britain during any month in the Battle of Britain – and Malta is just 15 miles long by 11 miles wide!

Then Spitfires did arrive. But initially they almost caused the morale of the island and its defenders to crack, for they were too few in number, many flown by inexperienced pilots and as their arrival was well known by the Germans, they were soon destroyed both in the air and on the ground. It was thought that if Spitfires could not save Malta, then nothing could. If there had been a glimmer of light at the end of the tunnel it was almost extinguished.

The Spitfire story will be dealt with later, but for now the Hurricane days were over. JG 26 had withdrawn from the fray but were replaced by units of JG 53. Muncheberg had gone, only to be replaced by Gerhard Michalski of II/JG 53. Some reckon he went on to shoot down even more RAF fighters over Malta than Muncheberg and Me 109 losses were still few.

Although official records show that barely 60 Hurricane pilots lost their lives over Malta, this is but a small part of the story. Many times more were shot down, baled out, and fought again, while others crash landed. Many others were wounded. Scores of Hurricanes were also lost on the ground. The figures tell the story. Of nearly 400 Hurricanes delivered to Malta by carrier, ship, or being flown in from France in 1940, by April 1942 it was hard to find one in fighting trim.

The Hurricanes didn't save Malta but they gallantly held the fort until better fighters could do so. Heroes among the Hurricane pilots were plentiful. The most successful of all was Sergeant Fred Robertson, whose Malta tally of victories numbered 10. Close behind were those two great characters, 'Ragbags' Rabagliati and 'Mac' MacLachlan (who lost his left arm over the island), while George Burges, the island's first defender, was credited with 7 air victories, a figure shared with another 261 Squadron pilot, Flying Officer Eric Taylor. The South African, Pilot Officer H P Lardner-Burke scored one less while at least half a dozen pilots also qualified as 'aces' with their five victories.

Amongst these was young David Barnwell, the son of the man who designed the Bristol Blenheim bomber; his victories were largely scored at night with the MNFU. 'Butch' Barton, a Canadian Squadron Leader and former Battle of Britain pilot, who led from the front, may have exceeded five enemy 'kills' while 'Timber' Woods and Flying Officer John Waters (who was the first to score in a Hurricane) both reached this figure. 261 Squadron alone claimed over 100 air victories and counted among their successful pilots, Sergeants Harry Ayre, Reg Hyde and Jim Pickering, Pilot Officers Hamish Hamilton, J Pain and A J Rippon.

They and their collegues, nevertheless, made a massive contribution, without which the Spitfires would have had no island to defend in 1942. It also had to be remembered that Malta took away from the Russian front one third of the Luftwaffe strength from before Moscow. Luftlotte II flew 11,574 sorties against Malta, which were sorties not flown against the Russians at a time when Russia was reeling!

CHAPTER TWO

GROUNDCREW

Of the many ground crew personnel who served so valiantly on Malta we here have two stories. One from Eddie Brind, another from Titch Holroyd. Eddie Brind arrived on the island in January 1941 when air raids were not too bothersome, but, as he puts it: 'Within days, all hell was let loose!' as the Illustrious Blitz had begun. About 30 airmen had arrived together, Eddie going to Luqa.

> Prior to the Blitz, Luqa was not too unlike other RAF stations, well laid out, reasonable billets... There was the usual bull shit and special police, not too many but a pain in the arse as always.

The famous G-shelter, which was to become the nerve centre of Luqa had been built deep underground and civilians were digging others. No 69 Squadron was the only regular user of the airfield and had its own maintenance crews, but Eddie was simply attached to Station Personnel.

During the Illustrious Blitz, the Germans dive bombed Luqa and life there was never the same again, although such attacks later became almost commonplace. When it came, Eddie and a bunch of others were in the showers, for they had just been given their first 12 hour pass and their first thought was to visit Valletta and see for themselves what the infamous 'Gut' – the street of low dives – was really like. Within minutes Eddie and his pals were trapped as the roof of the showers was blown away, with hot shrapnel, instead of hot water, raining down. Breaking through a jammed door they managed to free themselves and ran to a half completed shelter, despite being almost 'starkers', as well as negotiating (somewhat carefully!) a barbed wire fence in the process. Eddie recalls

> I was wet with fright as well as water, and two photographers who were taking pictures received a direct hit, a sight which shook us up a bit.

By the end of the raid the airfield was a shambles. Billets were smashed, kit had been destroyed or buried. Dressing in whatever could be found they were taken to Kalafrana for new kit, then back to Luqa to help clear up the mess. That was the end of their first day off on Malta.

The airmen on Luqa began to call themselves the Luqa Harriers, for during air raids a lorry would rush round dispersal areas to pick up the men and rush them to shelters. Obviously the lorry driver didn't linger over long and many had to race to catch it. One airman in fact, missed it but still managed to beat the lorry to the shelter. Eddie is convinced that he'd witnessed the first four minute mile! It was not long before slit-trenches were dug around the dispersal areas.

Eddie remembers night raids too as Ju 88s infiltrated the circuit in order to attack incoming transit aircraft en route to Egypt. A few 109s were also liable to fly in low in daylight to strafe the field. Aircraft losses on the ground were considerable as not all aircraft had been yet provided with anti-blast pens.

> The Duty Crew at night had a hectic time too. There was no electric flare-path so emergency Goose-neck flares had to be used, lit one by one, while a row of hurricane lamps were placed to delineate the threshold. An ancient Crossley truck, which lacked a good clutch and had no top gear, was used. Jerry would wait until all were lit, then come down and shoot up the new arrivals, or anything else that moved, and to plaster the place with delayed action and anti-personnel bombs. So unpopular did the job become that for punishments, flare-path duty was handed out instead of 'Jankers.'

Another unpopular job was burial party – an all too frequent event – made more unpleasant because the cemetery was close to the dockyard which was bombed frequently. On one occasion dive bombers began streaming down and the officers, a flight sergeant, two corporals and the padre, all took one look at the diving aircraft and smartly leapt into the open grave, while the firing party blazed away with their rifles; intended to be used in the farewell salute!

* * *

There were more popular diversions, among them some pleasant clubs in Valletta where one could relax. 'Vernons', where one could have a haircut, shave, hot towel and steaming bath, and the Opera

House tea dances. Then there was the British Institute, an excellent place to meet local Maltese girls. The well known 'Gut' was a sleazy area – out of bounds to officers. Its real name was Straight Street.

It wasn't too rough at the top end but the further you went down hill towards the waterfront, the less respectable it got. There, a Gents toilet was apt to be a tin bucket behind a rough screen of canvas. Such places abounded with female 'sherry bandits'. They expected fees for favours and for each dance you had to buy them a so called sherry. In another bar a couple of 'queers' – Sugar and Billy – did a much applauded cabaret turn.

As evenings in the Gut progressed, fights would break out as the alcohol filtered through. Army versus Navy; RAF versus Army; Maltese versus Brits, etc. It was something like the Wild West pictures, but you could sleep it off at a number of establishments which provided bed with early morning tea for only a shilling a night – with shoes and cap badge cleaned.

As the bombing increased with the return of the Luftwaffe in late 1941, the loss of aircraft was so great that by April 1942 all bombers had been removed save for the Special Duties Flight (of which more later). Ground crew losses were also fairly frequent as, when work was to be done, the men stayed on the job until the very last minute, carrying on until seeing enemy aircraft right overhead or already diving.

Eddie once made the mistake, as others did, of confusing Macchi 202 fighters for Hurricanes, both types looking alike. When a flight of six appeared, he stood and cheered, thinking that a new batch of Hurricanes was being flown in but when they began to open fire:

We hit the deck, cursing Mussolini, but after a change of underpants we carried on working. The raid cost us a couple of aircraft for no loss to the Regia Aeronautica.

Like almost every other serviceman, Eddie went down with the dreaded 'Malta Dog'- a local version of dysentery. He also contracted skin complaints and had to have a vast carbuncle on his neck lanced – still carrying the scar to this day.

When the Spitfires arrived some were based at Luqa and Eddie Brind enjoyed working on those renowned fighters. In fact he played a part in the brilliant ground organisation which, on 9 May, 1942, saved the island and enabled the Spitfires to be rearmed, refuelled and sent off to tackle the Luftwaffe, all within ten minutes of landing from the American carrier *Wasp* and the British carrier *Eagle*.

Each Spitfire was immediately guided to a pen which had been stocked with all that was required for a rapid turn round. The long-range tank was whipped off, armourers rearmed the planes as necessary while a gang of refuellers – often all army – would fill the tanks from a long line of 4 gallon tins. Meantime, mechanics would see to engines, clean windscreens, check radio and electrical equipment and so on. Standing ready was a battle hardened veteran of the Malta skies to replace the ferry pilot who had flown in the fighter. The revenge those Spitfires inflicted upon the enemy was sweet. The troops all cheered when the Ju 87s and Ju 88s started tumbling out of the skies. Morale had also been lifted by the cigarettes delivered, unofficially, by the pilots in transit aircraft.

Eddie also pays a special tribute to the Royal Navy men who managed to keep Malta alive by bringing in supplies via the fast minelayers, such as *Manxman*, *Welshman*, and the submarines *Thunderbolt* (ex *Thetis*), *Clyde*, *Severn*, and others.

But the enemy were always thinking up new ways to menace the defenders. Hatred of them rose when the 'butterfly' anti-personnel bombs were dropped. Some looked like tins of Machonochie's stew and airman were killed or maimed when having a kick at them. If touched they generally exploded, although Powell-Shedden actually picked up two and threw them into the notorious quarry at the end of the down hill runway where so many aircraft had come to grief. For reasons which can't be explained, neither went off.

* * *

Eddie Brind's interest in rebuilding aircraft was well appreciated during a spell when he was posted to Kalafrana where the main RAF workshops stood. They were a vital part of the island's hopes of survival and kept a low profile so as not to be attacked, which it wasn't much of the time.

When repaired, the aircraft would be pushed or driven in a special truck up the hill about a mile, to the FAA's Hal Far airfield where they would be test flown. On one occasion when the sirens went, Eddie was with the truck driver who drove to a nearby village for safety. The rest of the men took shelter in a ferro concrete shelter near Flying Control. It received a direct hit. All his mates perished.

On another occasion during a heavy raid, the Torpedo Dept blew up. Eddie was in a shelter which was blown down, the occupants being buried and trapped for some hours.

Things were not very pleasant and the Maltese were giving their rosaries a real bashing and praying to every Saint in the book. Many MT and engineering friends of mine were killed in the raid as well as the entire torpedo section and some special police. Bill, a corporal friend of mine, was not found at all and it was presumed that he had been blown to bits until a mongrel dog he had befriended, started worrying at a huge hangar door which had been blown down. When they lifted it, there was the remains of Bill.

Looking back, I feel it was a great privilege to serve with the Luqa Harriers and I sometimes felt that I had been on the island in a previous age.

* * *

Tich Holroyd, a Yorkshiremen, will also never forget his 2 plus years on Malta, although at the time he would willingly have exchanged them for almost anything elsewhere. He had arrived on the island aboard the *Manxman* and was assigned to RAF Ta Kali. Like all men who worked at Ta Kali, they thought they had the worst of it, then so too did the men who worked at Hal Far or Luqa. He had the lull following the Luftwaffe's move to Russia but knew all about Italian propaganda. Often he would see Italian bombers dropping their bombs into the sea and later hear fantastic claims over Italian radio. One day they claimed terrible destruction of the 'marshalling yards at Filfola.' Since Malta had no railway system and Filfola is only an uninhabited rock off the SW coast, the claim was a curious one! But there were some Italian pilots who seemed exceptionally brave and even accurate. On those occasions they would attack in a vic of three or five with complete disregard for fighters or AA fire, even when one of the vic had been hit and shot out of the formation.

One of Tich's first tasks was to help check some Hurricanes and get them into good fighting trim. No sooner had this been done than the Italians dropped a stick of bombs across the area and more or less wrote off the whole lot. Food initially was sufficient but lacked variety. The inevitable Machonichie's tinned stew, some bully beef, with local lettuce and tomatoes; the NAAFI was a help too. There was even free rations of cigarettes – about 50 a week at one peak time – and chocolate of a very hard variety.

During the invasion scare, Tich recalls three sergeants from the Royal Irish Fusiliers and Manchesters came to the airfield to put the airmen through their paces and teach them about airfield defence. There was no love lost either way. On one occasion, an airmen palmed a safety pin of a hand grenade which he then showed to one of the NCO's and innocently asked what he should do now that he had put the detonator in and pulled out the pin? To everyone's amusement, the sergeant instructor was the first to dive out of the building.

During bayonet drill and unarmed combat, Tich, due to his size, was often singled out for demonstrations of unarmed combat. He got tired of this and having earlier been in the LDV (later Home Guard), knew about bayonet drill and the answers to some attacks. When next the sergeant came at him, Tich dropped on one knee but with his rifle butt on the ground, the bayonet pointing upwards. The blade missed the sergeant's throat by inches. 'He went white as a sheet,' says Tich, 'but never again called me out for his demonstrations.'

Like everyone else at Ta Kali, Tich remembers the blitz of 20 March, 1942. It began at 5.45 in the afternoon and really flattened the place. The camp was almost destroyed and the men scattered around the villages. By this time the lack of food had become a major problem; accommodation too. With the arrival of the Spitfires and more pilots, Tich lost his tent. He teamed up with Bill Metcalf who had a stray dog whom they named Cherry. Cherry slept between them for comfort but was simply covered in fleas. They wiped the animal down with a petrol-soaked rag and the fleas poured out in hundreds! (see also Chapter 14).

To help with the food, the rations were augmented with some form of hard-tack biscuits. Attempts to make these more palatable by grinding them up and mixing them with bits of figs, chocolate, tomato, etc, failed. Then Tich had a go, steaming the porridge like mess, using the Times of Malta newspaper instead of greaseproof paper. It worked, was declared 'marvellous' and henceforth Tich became chief 'duff-maker.'

Luck also played a part in men's survival and so it did for Tich. When servicing a Beaufighter, the Warrant Officer came to advise him of a pay parade. The job was urgent and all but finished. Tich wanted to complete the run-up first but the Warrant Officer was having none of it. So off Tich and the others went. During their brief absence, a bomb came and demolished the pen and the Beau.

I would have been in it running the engines and would not have heard the warning alarm. At least four of us would have been killed for sure.

Another task for the Beaus was to carry Very Top Brass to high level meetings in the Middle East. Quite a few passengers could squeeze into the back of a Beau. Among others he can recall strapping in, were the AOC, Keith Park, and the Governor of Malta, Lord Gort VC. Tich did his best to show Gort how to use a parachute but Gort seemed fatalistic. 'I won't get the hang of it,' he said finally.

Not only food, but clothes were in short supply. Tich remembers strapping a squadron leader into a Spitfire, the man having no shirt but just a tie! He had probably left it behind to get washed, and didn't have a spare.

While Tich was with Beaufighters he got very attached to his 272 Squadron aeroplanes and thought the world of the unit's dynamic leader, Wing Commander J K Buchanan.

Conditions noticeably improved after the successful invasion of Sicily in 1943 but it was not until January 1944 that Tich Holroyd finally left the island. It is no wonder that he now says he can never forget those days – nor would want to. Listening to his stories has been a memorable experience, not to be forgotten.

CHAPTER THREE

THE FLEET AIR ARM

Not so well known is the important role in the air activities from Malta played by the crews of the Fleet Air Arm; from the very beginning to the bitter end. The Royal Navy of course was no stranger to Malta but in the beginning it was pure chance that led to 830 Squadron of the FAA being on Malta at all. Chance and the weather at Bordeaux.

For some months in early 1940, the FAA had maintained a training squadron, known as 767 T Squadron at Polyvestre in the south of France, working with the old aircraft carrier *HMS Argus*, teaching pilots the art of deck landing with the Fairey Swordfish. It was still there in May 1940 when the German assault in the west began, and by the time Paris fell and Italy had entered the war, 767 Squadron's position became precarious. The Admiralty immediately ordered it to fly the aircraft to Bordeaux which was still in Allied hands; but if the weather seemed uncertain, the Swordfish should be flown to Bone, Algeria. As the weather at Bordeaux was reported to be foggy, the Swordfish crews took themselves off to Bone, which was fortunate, as Bordeaux had been taken by the Germans!

The refuge in North Africa was brief. Following France's surrender 767 Squadron had to get away quickly. There were not many places to go but Malta was handy, so a dozen of the biplanes were flown to the island to form 830 Squadron, while the rest flew to Gibraltar.

Few squadrons could have had more dramatic birth pangs, nor were their troubles over in arriving at Hal Far airfield. With Malta an obvious threat to Mussolini's much publicised Naval power, the island was already under threat and attack by the Italian air force. Hal Far was barely operational and, not unnaturally, the Services on Malta had not been informed that the Swordfish would be arriving. Moreover, when they did arrive, it was in the middle of an air raid and the airfield was littered with cars and buses to avoid the possibility of an invasion! Luckily with the slow landing speeds of the Swordfish, the pilots got all the aircraft down without mishap, but all the ground personnel were absent: all down in the air raid shelters.

Other than the handful of Gladiators, the Swordfish Squadron found themselves to be almost the entire air force on Malta. For a few days the crews settled in, found comfortable quarters but within a week the Mess at Hal Far had been demolished. This started the pattern for the next couple of years, trying to find somewhere to live and finding some unbombed portion of the airfield on which to land. In the hands of its dedicated aircrews, 830 Squadron – usually operating out of Hal Far, that small airfield on the southern tip of Malta – were to achieve miracles during their period on the island. When Hal Far was out of action due to enemy action or rain churning its surface into a muddy morass, the Swordfish would transfer to nearby Luqa. Later these two airfields would be joined together by a long, tortuous taxi track which roamed this way and that, uphill and downhill as it circumvented bomb craters and quarries. In between was Safi Strip which, for most of its early life was merely a connecting link between the two airfields of Luqa and Hal Far. Only later in the war did a section of it become Safi flying strip. Until then it gradually filled up with damaged or written off aircraft: one of the air forces' graveyards for wrecked aeroplanes.

Initially, 830 Squadron and its 'Stringbags' as all affectionately came to call their aircraft, were used as dive bombers! Their first assignments being to attack the Sicilian port of Augusta where the Italians kept most of their submarine fleet. The Stringbag could carry three 500lb bombs as well as some much smaller, often incendiary bombs. Trained to drop torpedoes, they had never dropped bombs until they went to Sicily. Operationally the Squadron was controlled by the underground RAF HQ in the 'Ditch' near Valletta.

* * *

On 13 September 1940, the shape of the war in the Mediterranean changed when the desert land armies in Egypt and Libya joined in battle. Libya and adjoining Tripolitania were both Italian colonies and on the 13th the Italians crossed over the Egyptian border bent on conquest. Overnight Malta's strategic importance was fully recognised.

From this date the Swordfish ceased to be dive-bombers, having lost two of their number with little to show for it, and reverted to their proper role as torpedo attack planes. Another important event was the arrival, in September 1940, of Squadron Leader E A 'Titch' Whiteley's 431 Flight RAF, consisting of three reconnaissance Maryland aircraft, (in January 1941, 431 Flight became 69 Squadron). From then on the island commanders had better means of finding out where the enemy ships might be, which, of course, was invaluable. One place the Flight kept under close observation, was Taranto, where the Italian fleet was based. Whiteley and his brilliant photographic pilot, Adrian Warburton, kept an eye on this and all other enemy bases and airfields.

The Swordfish crews of 830 Squadron were keen to try their hand at any form of hostile operation, even laying mines outside the harbour of Tripoli on the African coast. They also dropped bombs on the town, flying sorties together with the first Wellington bomber unit on Malta – 148 Squadron.

Luqa was now fully operational and the Wellingtons also operated from there because of its long runways. When the *Illustrious* staggered into Valletta badly damaged, Hal Far was reinforced with six Fulmer fighters from the carrier, plus seven of the ship's Swordfish – a welcome addition to the FAA's total force. Torpedo attacks, by 1941, were being regularly carried out. The first to hit a ship with a torpedo was Sub-Lieutenant Potts-Dawson on 27 January. The 3,950 ton German merchantman *Ingo* going to the bottom.

The Squadron was now a tough, well knit unit with a number of skills learnt the hard way. The *Ingo* was just the first of many ships sunk by the Stringbags, especially after the arrival of the Marylands. The Fulmars too, calling themselves 800X Squadron, started night intruder sorties against Sicilian airfields.

The enemy ships could be stopped by aircraft only by bombing or by torpedo strike. The brave Blenheim crews, operating in daylight, carried the main burden for the former, while 830 Squadron was for a long time the only unit operating with the torpedo. There was, of course, also the Royal Navy operating from Malta. Their remarkable Force-K, two light cruisers *Aurora* and *Penelope* and their two small destroyers, *Lance* and *Lively*, achieved wonders under Captain Bill Agnew's inspired leadership. They once wiped out an entire convoy of seven ships and sank all bar one of its escorts. In all they sank about a dozen ships without as much as a single casualty to themselves.

The Navy also kept a small flotilla of submarines in Manoel

Island, Lazaretto Creek. They too achieved great success also against enormous odds. If Commander M D Wanklyn VC DSO DSC, in *Upholder*, was their star with 21 ships sunk, including two destroyers, three submarines, three big troop transports, two tankers and ten other supply vessels, others also had splendid records, notably *Urge, Upright, Unbeaten* and *Unique*. In all the nine tiny 'U' class British submarines sent about 350,000 tons of enemy shipping to the bottom – over 60 ships in all.

To achieve all these successes the RAF and Navy worked in almost perfect unison. Both used the same information and every strike was made in conjunction with the sister service. Their two leaders, Hugh Pughe Lloyd and Vice Admiral Ford thought and acted as one, from their adjacent operations rooms in the underground area commonly known as 'The Ditch' or 'The Hole'.

As it was difficult – ie: suicidal – for 100 mph biplanes to attack shipping in daylight, virtually all Swordfish attacks had to be made at night. Realising this, the enemy made sure its ships passed closest to Malta during daylight. Squadron Commander F D Howie, CO of 830 Squadron, set about the novel task of finding and attacking ships at night. The problem of finding them was never adequately solved until ASV (Air to Surface Vessel) radar equipped aircraft could be employed; and at first there were none. Later when these did become available the tactics were to take-off individually and form up into a tight formation by arranging to meet over the rock Filfola, close to the southern tip of the island or by circling a flame float which the leader would drop off shore. Only the leading plane would carry a navigator, the others formated on him.

In finding the enemy ships, which was never easy in the dark even when aided by ASV, much would have to depend on whether there was a friendly moon. An attack into a moon path had many advantages. The ship would be silhouetted and the attacker would be approaching from the dark side of the sky. Not that the enemy sailed past Malta on such occasions without a very good reason, for the stars and moonshine are very bright in the Mediterranean. Thus it was usual for the leader to drop flares on one side of the convoy while the other aircraft attacked from the dark side. All of which required a good deal of exact timing and practice.

The Squadron also suffered due to the arguments between the Admiralty and Admiral Sir Andrew Cunningham, C-in-C the Navy at Alexandria. The former preferred mining of harbours which Cunningham thought a hit and miss affair while the latter put his faith in the torpedo.

Reinforcements arrived in July 1940 with the arrival of six Swordfish from the *Ark Royal*, one or two of which were equipped with Mark I ASV – even if by later standards it was a crude affair. At about the same time, Charles Lamb, a very experienced Swordfish pilot and former flight commander aboard the *Illustrious* joined Hal Far's force. Although not in command, Lamb seems to have been briefed to take whatever actions were required to ensure that 830 remained on the offensive, although at first he grounded everyone until night-flying panels were fitted to the aircraft.

The Swordfish pilots also received some information about ship sailings via brave agents operating clandestine wireless sets behind enemy lines. In North Africa they were based in Tunisia, where a Swordfish would land one on a dried-up lake bed and pick up the previous one. Unfortunately, Lamb, flying one of these dangerous missions, discovered the lake bed not wholly dry and the Swordfish tipped over on landing. He and Sub Lieutenant J M Robertson, his observer, were handed over to the French: Tunisia then being a (neutral) French colony.

Meantime, other experienced crews had arrived on the island, coming from the damaged carrier *Formidable*, from which they had been involved in the successful Battle of Matapan. Among them were R Edgar Bibby, G M T 'Woozle' Osborne, Williams, H E H 'Pancho' Pain and the South African, F C Nottingham. Lieutenant Commander Howie left Malta in August 1941, having received a richly deserved DSO. Later his place was taken by Lieutenant Commander J G Hunt, another observer.

Meanwhile, the bearded Pancho Pain took temporary command and during his spell in charge, the tactics of co-operating with the ASV Wellingtons of the Special Duties Flight (SDF) were developed. Although a couple of the Swordfish now carried ASV, they still lacked the range for any prolonged search for the elusive enemy, whereas the Wellingtons could search for hours. The Wimpys of the SDF had been flown to Malta specifically to locate enemy ships at sea at night so that others might be guided to an attack. The SDF and the FAA worked well together and whenever a Swordfish scored a success, they would be debriefed in person by Hugh Pughe himself who would reward the kill by handing over a rare bottle of gin.

Following the initial success, further successes came over the next months, the Stringbags being responsible for the loss of the enemy's ships: –*Juventus, Sparta, Brarena, Punaco, California, Maddalena Ordero, Egardi, Rialto, Poadesta, Bainsizza, Perla, Caterina*, plus a number of unidentified ships. All were hit by the Swordfish although in some instances the coup-de-grace to a damaged ship was delivered by either a submarine or a Luqa based Blenheim. In addition to the above named men, the following – mainly lieutenants – were all involved in these attacks. A S Whitworth, W F C Garthwaite, R G Lawson, P Cotton, Stew Campbell, J R O Stevenson and N K Campbell. Later arrivals were Pat E H O'Brien, Taylor, C R J Coxon, Walsh, Gillingham and R E F Kerrison.

The last named must have thought the Gods were against him. En-route to the Middle East his ship was sunk and he was severely injured and soon after being released from hospital he was involved in a mid-air collision! Fit once more he was sent to Malta in a Sunderland, only to be shot up and shaken up in the crash landing. No sooner had he started ops from Hal Far than the engine of his Swordfish failed and he had to ditch and spend the night in a dinghy. However, he finally got his chance to shine, and in conjunction with a SDF Wellington in December 1941, played a major part in the sinking of the 1,235 ton tanker, *Lina*, as well as having put a torpedo into the cruiser *Duca degli Abruzzi* the previous month.

Lieutenant Commander Hunt arrived in early November, an officer senior to Pain although with less Malta experience. On the 11th, he decided to lead and navigate a strike force of seven Swordfish (flying in Lieutenant Osborne's aircraft) against a ship the SDF had found west of the island in the Lampedusa-Pantellaria area. The weather was bad and soon after take-off three of the torpedo planes had to abort, luckily for them, for the others were not heard of again for several years.

The new CO led his flock into a situation from which there was no escape. When in a position between Sardinia and Sicily, well over 100 miles off course, and with insufficient fuel to get back, Myles Osborn took over the lead and headed south east until they had the northern coast of Sicily in sight. There he instructed everyone to jettison their torpedoes and ditch close to shore, Stewart Campbell actually sending his torpedo in the direction of Palermo before ditching. Three of the crews were successful but Lieutenant A F Wigram and his gunner, Leading Aircraftman K D Griffiths, were lost.

Campbell was later shot up in his dinghy which was holed, forcing him and his gunner to swim to shore. Two years later he managed to escape from captivity and it was only then that the story of what had happened emerged.

As it happens, I was the pilot of the SDF Wellington, and I continued to shadow the ship, wondering why no Swordfish appeared. I surmised that the wind must have changed and the Swordfish had turned back and run out of petrol. Searches were made but obviously, nobody even thought of looking to the north of Sicily.

Lieutenant Commander Myles Osborne DSO DSC, who knew this was his last sortie from Malta, having been ordered to the US Naval Air Station, Pensacola, Florida, as an instructor, relates:

> About halfway to Lampedusa, the CO had given me an ETA and announced that the wind had changed and was now blowing from the north west. My experience warned me to query this very large change, evoking the curt comment to mind my own business.
>
> An hour or so later 1 saw, through the murk, the shape of an island, drew the attention of the CO, who gave me a new course for Pantelleria. I noticed that we were a long time passing Lampedusa and then recalled that our theoretical ground speed had been reduced by at least 30 knots following the shift in the wind. My thoughts were rudely interrupted when the CO announced that our ASV had ceased to function, which meant that the strike force was entirely dependant on the Wellington to locate the convoy.
>
> We flew on and when we were halfway to the ETA at Pantelleria, I told the CO I would be happier if we got a radio fix from Malta but he replied that it was unnecessary. Later I was not entirely surprised when this ETA came and went without sighting the island. After intimating my concern to the CO several times he reluctantly agreed to raise Malta on the W/T, but despite the efforts of all four radio operators there was no response from base.
>
> I asked the CO where he thought we might be and after a long pause he hazarded the Bay of Sfax – over 200 miles SSW of Pantelleria and rather more than Malta! I

disconnected the Gosport tube to think things out without interruption, realizing that we were in one hell of a situation – lost, with three relatively inexperienced pilots and crews with the prospect of ditching in heavy seas close to an enemy shore. I took the formation down to 100 feet and found the wind blowing strongly from the south east and on the assumption that the wind had 'not' changed direction since take-off, I analyzed our progress stage by stage.

I finally deduced that our first landfall was in fact Pantelleria and we were now heading for Sardinia in the latitude well to the north of Sicily and had been airborne for more than 3 hours. I informed the CO but he showed no interest, nor made any suggestions. If my calculations were right, we had no chance of reaching Malta, some 300 miles away. Accordingly I turned ESE with the expectation of sighting the north east coast of Sicily and in fact my first sighting was one of the Lipari islands. I turned south and later with a young moon and improved visibility, saw a coast line running east/west.

Some five miles from the coast, with something less than 20 minutes flying time left, I signalled jettison torpedoes and asked the CO to do the same with the ASV set, which entailed loosening four butterfly nuts, lifting it up and dropping it over the side, but for reasons unknown he was unable to do this.

As we neared the shore I noticed some cliffs to port and a beach to starboard, with what appeared to be a dry salt lake about a mile inland. Any thought of landing was ended when flak came up so we reformed over a flame float out to sea. A further request to the CO to dump the ASV set was again unsuccessful. About three miles out we ditched and got into the dinghy. An aircraft then passed overhead and shortly afterwards saw a flash and heard the faint sound of an explosion which appeared later to be Lt Wigram who most likely hit a rock and blew up.

It was now crucial to draw attention to our predicament and asked the CO for the Very pistol but he replied that he had left it in the cockpit when he thought he might have to swim for the shore. I was beside myself and could barely contain my anger at this display of unprofessionalism, placing us once again in a dangerous situation.

With no paddles it was an exhausting business using just our hands and then a machine gun opened up on us and we dived over the side but once the dinghy was out of the moon path the firing stopped and we got back in. We were then able to get within a mile or so of the shore but the wind changed at dawn and by 10 o'clock we were some ten miles out to sea.

In the afternoon they were picked up by a trawler and taken – on piggy back – ashore at Cefalu, to start more than 3 years as prisoners. Later Osborne discovered that although Wingram and his gunner Griffiths had died, Stew Campbell and Taylor with their rear men, Fallon and Robinson had all got ashore safely.

* * *

The Swordfish Squadron were understandably subdued after this incident but the arrival of Lieutenant Commander F H E (Frank) Hopkins as new CO rapidly restored the status quo and confidence returned.

Not that 830 were entirely alone now, for just before the tragic loss of the four crews, 828 Squadron FAA had arrived in mid-October, equipped with Albacores – known generally as 'Applecores'! Unfortunately the Albacore's Bristol Taurus engine proved less reliable than the old Pegasus and as an aircraft it was far less easy to keep serviceable. Their arrival coincided with that of the Germans so they had little time or opportunity for practice and within days too, their aircraft were being damaged in air attacks. Then their CO, Lieutenant Commander D E Langmore was lost in action and the Squadron became so depleted that finally the remnants of the two Squadrons were amalgamated into one unit, called the Royal Naval Air Squadron – Malta.

Another further development in the battle for North Africa was that Rommel took the port of Tobruk, so the enemy ships could now take routes which were seldom within range of the torpedo planes. An occasional torpedo attack was made possible and early in 1942 Albacores flown by Lieutenant P C Whitfield and others, guided to a target by the SDF, claimed hits upon an Italian cruiser, and Lieutenant J B Blakeley hit a tanker – a prize target. In June

1942, a force from the hybrid unit attacked – in daylight – elements of the Italian battle fleet while under attack from Beauforts from both Malta and the Middle East. However, the heyday of the torpedo biplanes on Malta had passed and not until the tide of battle in North Africa turned and the Axis forces were in retreat in Tunisia did targets once more become available to them. But then the hybrid unit was disbanded as new units arrived at Hal Far.

No 821 Squadron (Albacores) flew in from North Africa following a successful period of dropping flares over targets being bombed by Wellingtons, and 828 Squadron came into its own once more, having been reformed in North Africa. Both units had several successes during the closing stages of the Tunisian battles, 828's last success being the sinking of the *Velino* in Syracuse harbour itself. Soon thereafter, its three remaining aircraft were handed over to 826 Squadron which arrived in Malta to carry on the good work.

No 830 Squadron of the Fleet Air Arm had been the very first air unit to arrive in Malta and to take the fight to the Italians. It succeeded in writing a glorious chapter in the history of its Service. It was also the first unit of that air arm to demolish the antiquated idea that only officer pilots/ observers could attack the enemy with torpedoes. 828 Squadron under most adverse conditions did its best to maintain the attack.

I myself, regard it a privilege to have been able to co-operate with such gallant men.

CHAPTER FOUR

GROUNDCREW II

It would be difficult to find more typical stories than those of Airmen Jim Somerville, Richard Slater or Alf Barnett. Few have written it down better than Jim. And it is not just that he explains it so well – 'How to fight a war with a few spanners and a couple of screwdrivers.'

During Jim's time on the island he had to endure several spells in Imtarfa Hospital; he had to shift his billet time and time again; he contracted 'Malta Dog', sand-fly fever, had a shrapnel injury, lost stones in weight during the famine and siege and lost nearly all his kit.

He worked at Hal Far, Ta Kali and Luqa and had some alarming near misses. He lost close mates in circumstances that, but for the will of God or luck of the draw, could so easily have been himself. He found himself well trained in normal maintenance but had to train himself how to service aircraft without spares by cannibalization – robbing 'A' to keep 'B' flying, or by rummaging about in damaged aircraft for spare parts. As if this was not enough he had to work phenomenally long hours and had to walk miles to work each day. On his first day, in April 1941, he was walking across Hal Far when

Suddenly the air raid siren sounded. Away up in the clear blue sky could be seen some small dots – high level Italian bombers – followed by the crump, crump, crump of exploding bombs.' When another warning sounded during the night, Jim followed the others into a shelter: 'Where the bombs fell I do not know, but it sounded as if each and every one was coming straight at the shelter. I felt more frightened underground than I was where I could see the sky, so was never in a shelter again.

Jim had reason to thank his lucky stars for this sensible decision. Quite apart from being able in future to watch interesting raids, if he bothered to do so, there soon came the day when he and some mates were walking from maintenance to the mess hall for lunch.

Half way across the airfield the alert sounded. Smithy, a special friend, and myself carried on to the dining hall while our companions went down the hole. Just beyond the dining hall was the Sick Bay with two medics standing by the door. The dining hall was empty so we helped ourselves to Machonichie's stew and were hardly into our meal when there were a couple of almighty bangs. The shelter had been hit by at least one bomb and where the Sick Bay had stood there was just a large hole, while the dining hall remained totally undamaged. We buried our friends at Bighi.

By the time the Spitfires arrived, Jim Somerville was at Ta Kali, the primary fighter airfield. He recalls

The Spitfire was a completely new animal to us, sent to Malta without spare parts so we were soon back to the cannibalization stage.

Jim singles out Flight Sergeant Spiers as being a tower of strength during the transition stage. The problem always was that no sooner had a Spitfire been repaired than it was damaged once more and the work had to start all over again.

Ta Kali was raided in great strength on 20/21 March 1942. Jim checked post-war records to discover that during that Friday and Saturday, enemy planes numbered 180, 150 and then 130 in three raids. The base was an awful mess and the Spitfires had to be diverted to Luqa whence Jim went – with his tool box – not to return until 3 April, by which time he was a corporal. But even on this day, 249 Squadron records that 60 tons of bombs fell on Ta Kali during a 16.45 raid, with a similar amount 45 minutes later. Then a few days on in the village of Mosta, where he was billeted, he was hit in the leg by a splinter from an exploding bomb, which put him into Imtarfa Hospital.

While Jim lingered in hospital, the disaster of the destruction of the first batch of Spitfires occurred. Within two or three days only about half a dozen remained in a combat ready state. These aircraft, so badly yearned for, had been promptly written off before they could make an impact. Then, with the threat of invasion in the air, Jim was released from hospital. He went to the armoury to pick up a rifle and ammunition to help defend the airfield. He was still limping from his injury but with his rifle he could scarcely wait for the next strafing attack:

I awaited the return of our planes from a scramble. Sure enough they were being chased home by enemy fighters. Goodness knows how many rounds of ammo I blasted off or if I ever hit anything but it was a great feeling to be doing something to pay back for the weeks I'd spent in Imtarfa. The war had become very personal to me.

It was like having Christmas and a birthday in one on 9 May when 60 Spitfires arrived from the *Wasp* and *Eagle*. They were turned round, refuelled and made ready to take the air within 15 minutes – with experienced Malta pilots at the controls.

To everyone, this seemed to be the turning point and the Maltese still refer to the 'Glorious Tenth of May' following the damage inflicted on the 9th and then the 10th by the Spitfires. It seemed as if the days of humiliation were over. A nightmare that seemed never ending had abruptly ceased.

During his time on the island his billet changed many times: Hal Far; a bug ridden old pottery at Ta Kali; some commandeered private dwellings at Mosta; in primitive conditions in and around a farm near Qrendi; in the Boschetto Gardens about a mile from Rabat – under canvas; various short stints at Luqa as well as Imtarfa hospital! He was also at St Edwards College, M'dina, during the period soon after the Spits arrived, when most airmen at Ta Kali were on duty from half an hour before dawn until dusk, with a three mile walk each way before commencing his marathon stint of duty – as long as 18 hours during midsummer. The big snag about St Edwards was that there were no blackout curtains so he had to learn to shave in the dark since no lights were permitted and he was on duty during every moment of daylight hours.

Jim Somerville also recalls the RAF's amazing bomb disposal officer. It is believed that, prior to being on Malta, he had received no formal instruction in this dangerous and demanding task. Flight Lieutenant (later Squadron Leader) H B H Dickinson was a real hero. He tackled everything that fell and failed to explode. Some were delayed action bombs, others – quite a few – were duds! After every raid he could be seen peering into craters, measuring depths and widths, marking out areas with red danger flags before hastening onto the next 'UXB' – Unexploded Bomb. He well deserved his George Cross, like so many, earned the hard way.

Jim saw the battles of August and September 1942. During the latter month Spitfires were being fitted with bomb racks in order to attack airfields on Sicily. Then again in October when Kesselring's men gave it one final effort. When Jim finally left the battered island he had received a Mention in Despatches, although the vast majority of these valiant ground crew members received nothing – not even a special clasp on a war or campaign medal to show where they'd been, or what they have done or endured. Although later, just to say one had been on Malta, was usually enough to bring wonderment to a person who had not been there.[1]

* * *

Richard Slater had been part of a draft of about 200 airmen mechanics who departed from Gourock, Scotland, in the cruiser *HMS Euryalus*, in September 1941. They had tropical kit but it was not until they were passing Gibraltar that they learnt of their destination. After Gib they became part of the escort to a convoy and experienced the usual air-sea battles to reach the besieged island.

His duty aboard ship was as part of a gun's crew. His particular job was to remove, as hastily as he could, the expended shell casings. They were large, hot and heavy. His new tropical kit became covered in oil and once even caught fire! It was an appropriate baptism for what was to come.

Once on Malta he was posted to Luqa, billeted in tents between the airfield and the Poor House-cum-leper colony! He was soon almost bitten to death by an assortment of bugs, centipedes, beetles and flies. Later he was given a stone billet but it was soon bombed and several of the lads killed. Moved to another this too was hit and another eight to ten chaps killed. He then found himself in the Poor House itself along with hundreds of others.

> We didn't actually share accommodation with the lepers, but the sight of them with their disfigured hands and faces was disturbing.

Like Jim Somerville, Richard and the others were issued with rifles and often blazed away at low flying enemy aircraft. They were never sure if they hit anything but it made them all feel better.

---

[1] In April 1992, the Malta Government redressed this omission and awarded 50th anniversary Malta Medals to the like of Jim Somerville.

At Luqa, Richard worked on aircraft which usually only came in at night, refuelling on their way to Egypt. The pressure to get them away before first light was great. On one occasion he worked 36 hours at a stretch. Food was already becoming progressively scarce and he recalls that one old tin of biscuits issued as part of a days ration, contained weevils.

However, we were hungry and still ate the biscuits!

One humourist described the weevils as extra protein! Tins of other foodstuffs were often marked with 'Not fit for human consumption after (a date)', which was often long past.

The airmen soon discovered the Germans seemed to work to a pattern. An early morning recce flight would come over and if it discovered that new planes had arrived in the night, they knew they were in for a pasting. On some occasions a plane would arrive, the crew would rest up during the day, then depart the next night. Losses on the ground forced a change to a quick turn round and another crew would fly them out.

To keep the planes flying it was necessary to bend a number of rules. It was quite normal, therefore, for an airman to take on the job of taxying aircraft to dispersal as soon as they had been fixed up. One day Richard was doing this when the Station Commander in his car, came alongside, gesticulating for him to stop. Richard was 'given a frightful bollocking' and told never to do it again. Some time later another Wellington needed to be taxied away as a matter of urgency. The Station Commander told Richard to find a pilot right away. None was available so Richard was ordered to move it himself. 'Can't do that, Sir. You told me that I would be on a charge if ever found taxying an aircraft again.' The CO broke into a grin – 'You win!'

Richard also recalls some strange incidents:

There was a pilot who twice returned to Malta with a serviceable plane while reporting some imaginary fault. It transpired that the aeroplane's serial numbers added up to 13! He was taken off flying duties but the plane then received a direct hit in its pen! On another occasion a pal and me had been repairing a Wellington but this mate then refused to accompany me on the usual air test. It was Friday the 13th! The plane took off and almost at once both engines cut and the crash landing reduced the machine to a wreck. All aboard were injured, some quite seriously but I wasn't too badly hurt.

Later, Richard was posted to 126 Squadron, coming under the command of the wonderful Flight Sergeant H G W Cagby. He was a strict but fair man and admired by all. He rightly received the BEM (for removing bombs from the vicinity of a burning aircraft) as well as several Mentions in Despatches. Cagby had rigged up some machine guns on a standard and he and the other men would blaze away at strafing Messerschmitts etc. This helped tremendously when ammo for the AA guns became rationed. On the occasion that one Me 109 pilot landed his damaged fighter on the airfield, it was Cagby who was the first to go out and disarm the man.

With the RAF men fighting back with machine guns they had salvaged from crashed aircraft, there were odd occasions during a strafing attack when the army and navy men would be servicing a Spitfire while the RAF lads were in their home made defence posts shooting away at the Messerschmitts and Macchis; often directed by an army officer!

Later Richard was made sergeant and, after the main blitz, he managed to bum a ride in a transit Wellington to Cairo when given a week's leave. From there he managed to hitch a lift to Tripoli where he contrived to get on a Hudson flying back to Malta with some Top Brass on board. His Station Commander on Malta had told Richard not to leave the island and it was him who stood waiting to greet the Brass who had flown in! Richard was among the first off and although the Group Captain eyed him, nothing was said. Enterprise was always welcome on Malta.

* * *

Alf Barnett, from Manchester, was another airman who remembers Sergeant Cagby as an inspiration to all those around him; also the home made defensive gunfire. One day Alf was having 'the works' from the camp barber when suddenly low flying Me 109s appeared and began to strafe the airfield. 'After our evasive action,' says Alf, 'the lather was everywhere except in the right place!' The lads had been issued with a machine gun and he expected them to shoot down any Messerschmitts while he was being shampooed and shaved. But this shave had been a bit too close!

One day Alf was caught in the middle of the Luqa airfield as he well remembers:

> The camp alert sounded. I appeared to be the only soul around – not even Flight Sergeant Cagby was visible – just me and them, oh dear! I looked skyward and there they were, a squadron of Stuka dive-bombers heading in my direction. I ran as fast as I could and jumped into a ditch. The Stukas seemed to come in a never ending stream. I watched them dive and the bombs in flight appeared to be heading straight at me. The screaming aircraft sound was like Hell let loose and I really thought this was the end. I said a prayer audibly to the one above, then, suddenly, after what had seemed an age – although it was but a few seconds – there was unbelievable quiet. Peace after the storm with dust everywhere. I extricated myself from the ditch and wandered back to my post, covered from head to foot in that Maltese dust.

Everyone lost friends on Malta and Alf was no exception.

> Ginger Clarke was also from Manchester, and a fearless work colleague. One day we had occasion to call at another depot. After a short wait we decided that it didn't need two of us, so I went back and waited for his return, but he never came back. Very sadly, Ginger was one of those who lost everything!

* * *

Peter Hewlett was a Special Duties Clerk, working in the Operations Room and was to spend his 21st birthday on the island. His job was to 'filter' the plots of aircraft and identify all blips as either friendly or hostile. It was hard work, requiring hours of concentration but he was in a unique position to know how big or small each raid was, even if he was relatively safe underground.

He also arrived in the September 1941 lull although the convoy he'd come with had had to battle their way through the Med; part of the cargo on his ship being petrol and ammunition! Once settled in he was billeted near Marsamaxetto Creek complete with bed bugs, which they discouraged by sticking the legs of the bed in small tins of paraffin. The other nocturnal irritation was the regular muffled sounds of depth charges being dropped in Valletta Harbour to discourage Italian midget submarines.

At first he found the food situation not too bad. One could still buy food in the shops – even cream cakes. By December, however, the weather had deteriorated, Ju 88s were coming over every few hours and the food situation was becoming critical.

Later, Peter was ordered to give a hand at Luqa by helping to build aircraft pens out of petrol tins filled with sand and rubble, and was able to see for himself what the airmen on the airfields had to put up with. Even after air raid sirens sounded the airmen continued working until a red Very light was fired to indicate immediate danger.

In February he moved to a billet in Valletta but was only there a few weeks. From his position in the filter room he judged that the raid of 7 April 1942 was one of the heaviest – over 300 bombers. Valletta seemed to be the target and the Opera House, the Castille (army HQ) and the St Andrew's Hostel, where he now lived, were all destroyed. Peter lost all his belongings.

One sadness for those who watched the radar plots was to see transit aircraft from Gibraltar heading for Sicily instead of Malta and not being able to stop them. The Italians did all they could, by using phoney radio calls and W/T bearings, to lure these aircraft astray.

One day Peter had to visit the ground radar station at Dingli, sited on top of the cliffs there. While there he watched Me 109s flying by, being able to look DOWN on them as they headed past.

Peter finally left the island after two and a half years. He had seen many amazing sights, not least the arrival of the sad remains of the Operation Pedestal convoy of mid-August 1942. When the damaged tanker *Ohio* was slowly brought into Valletta many people were past cheering; they just stood with tears in their eyes.

The Royal Navy had lost an aircraft carrier, three cruisers and twelve destroyers in the June and August convoys, with another carrier, seven cruisers, four destroyers and a corvette damaged. In all 31 cargo ships had run the gauntlet of submarine and air attack and only four had arrived at Malta undamaged. Those ships and their cargo saved Malta.

CHAPTER FIVE

LUQA'S SIXTY NINE

Certain squadrons are identified with certain airfields. Mention Hal Far to anyone who was in Malta in 1940–42 and 830 Squadron of the FAA will come to mind. Mention Luqa at any time during the blitz and 69 Squadron springs to mind. It was born there out of 431 Flight and stayed to see Malta through all its troubles.

It was a photo-reconnaissance squadron which did what it could with whatever aircraft it could lay its hands on. It used Marylands, Blenheims, Beauforts, a Mosquito, Hurricanes, Wellingtons, Baltimores, Spitfires galore and even a FAA Skua. It was commanded by Australians, New Zealanders, a South African Captain, a British Wing Commander – holder of the rare George Cross, a Marine Captain, a Pilot Officer, several other Wing Commanders and, of course, by Adrian Warburton.

It all started when three US Glen-Martin Marylands were flown across occupied Europe to arrive in Malta in September 1940. Under their talented 'workaholic', Australian E A 'Tick' Whiteley, they at once began to supply the RAF and RN on the island with almost daily photographs of the enemy's ports and airfields. Soon they began to find and shadow ships operating between Sicily, Italy and the North African coast.

Two restrictions initially plagued them. They only had three aircraft with precious few spare parts and they only had three crews. Another problem was that the Maryland[1] was a new aeroplane to the RAF with few people who knew much about them, but Whiteley had had the good sense to choose his Wireless Operator/Air Gunner wisely. Corporal John Shephard was a very able ground electrician, and Whitley himself a brilliant mechanic.

At first the crews themselves did much of the servicing under Tich's guidance and John's instruction. It was fortunate that two of the navigators were also qualified pilots, although Warburton, who

---

[1] It was an American aircraft built by the Glenn Martin Co. The type was never ordered by the British but the French (and the South Africans) had placed small orders. With the fall of France, Britain took over the French order for use by the RAF.

was one of them, had never flown a Maryland before. Not surprisingly he all but wrote off one in Malta while attempting, without dual instruction, to master this quite sophisticated American type. The airfield boundary fence also suffered! It has also to be said that Warburton had not been a favourite of his former CO when on a squadron in England and, as soon as he was able to post Warburton overseas, that CO had been a much happier man.

When lack of spares proved a problem, Tich managed to persuade the AOC to waylay a couple of transit Blenheims for his use, which, incidently, set another pattern which, in the months ahead, did much to keep Malta operational; much to the chagrin of commanders in various parts of the Middle East who were themselves waiting for new aircraft.

Versatility was well known on Malta. When hydraulic fluid for the Marylands ran out, Tich, in company with George Burges, the former Gladiator Flight leader, now a flight commander on 69, manufactured a substitute from castor oil which was obtained from the nurses at a hospital in exchange for lipstick cunningly brought in from the UK. Tich's resourcefulness seems to have been unlimited. When they used up their supply of tail wheel tyres, he used thick rope instead!

The highly successful Taranto attack on 11 November, 1940, which changed the whole balance of naval power in the Mediterranean, put 69 Squadron in the history books. Their almost daily photo-recce of that port during the period immediately prior to the Swordfish aircraft's attack from *HMS Illustrious*, made it possible. Whiteley and Warburton were among the pilots involved; also 'Warby's' brilliant visual report on an occasion when photographs could not be taken. In his log-book he simply states for that sortie – 'Recce of Taranto', but his crew recount how he went in low around and inside the harbour to count the ships and note their positions! In all there were five battleships, 14 cruisers and (not all counted by Warby) 27 destroyers. After being chased away by Italian fighters the crew could not agree on totals, so Warburton went back in to do it all over again despite the defences now being well alert.

In the year that followed, 69 Squadron established a fine name for itself. The supply of Marylands was always critical and of the ten or so which they did obtain, all were eventually either destroyed on the ground or in the air. So they took over Hurricanes, stripped out the guns and installed cameras. George Burges helped with this and in his hands the converted day fighter could reach 36,000 feet – stupendous for a Mark I Hurricane. It was painted blue and known as Burges Blue Bastard.

When 69, formally 431 Flight, was made up to a full squadron there came the promise of 12 Marylands and 12 Beauforts but these never materialised. Nevertheless, with whatever aircraft it used, the Squadron brought back invaluable photos, ships were found, reported and shadowed. Whiteley himself found a convoy of five merchant ships and three destroyers on 15 April, 1941. Captain P J Mack with the 14th Flotilla of four destroyers then came out and sank the lot that night.

The Maryland was quite well armed with both front and rear guns. Warburton and his gunner, Paddy Moran, were particularly successful in attacking enemy aircraft, or defending themselves. Paddy and his skipper shot down at least five, possibly eight, including flying boats and fighters!

To supplement the official RAF high level cameras, the crews took to carrying Leica and other hand-held cameras to use when the clouds were low. The crews' determination to obtain photos knew no bounds. Warburton once came back with point blank photos of ships, identified by their names being readable. He also had the aerial from a cruiser wrapped round his tail wheel! On another occasion he even managed to get a handheld shot with a Leica when he strafed an airfield from 20 feet. Unofficial one man bombing raids were another 'extra' but having no bomb racks, the Wireless Operator/ Air Gunner had to kick out 25lb bombs through the open rear hatch!

Once the Luftwaffe were entrenched in Sicily, the crews found themselves being chased by the deadly efficient Me 109s. Their best chance to avoid destruction by these 109s was to fly in tight circles around known Malta AA gun sites. Wing Commander J N Dowland GC, who commanded the Squadron from September 1941 to January 1942, fought a long duel with one 109 in full view of the local populace. He escaped by superb handling but eventually had to crash-land in a bay off shore when low on fuel. Dowland and his gunner were then attacked in the water and killed. The other crewman baled out over the island with the precious photographs. The gunner, Bob Grindley, had been wounded in the air and probably was unable to get out of his turret. His son was born to his Maltese mother a day or so later. Earlier, on 20

November 1941, Dowland had had to bale out of a Hurricane, while encountering a Mc202, but was rescued from the sea.

A month later Me109s shot down two Marylands. On 15 February, Squadron Leader W E M Lowrey suffered engine failure on a mission and was then attacked by four Me 109s. Although two of the attackers were claimed as Probables, the Maryland was damaged but got away. Arriving back at Malta it was attacked again by 109s the damaged starboard engine being hit once more, forcing Lowrey to ditch in Kalafrana Bay, but the crew survived despite one of the 109 pilots trying to strafe them. Another Maryland, flown by Flight Lieutenant R J S Wootton, was coming to the island after repairs in Egypt. It ran into some 109s and was shot down. Bad weather then prevented a rescue attempt so the crew were lost.

In January 1942, Warburton, who had been, supposedly, 'on rest' in the Middle East, returned to Malta with a Beaufighter which had been converted for PR work. They had taken a ton and a half out of it – or so Warby said, and that in its now unarmed and unarmoured state, it could outrun anything flying in the area. Flight Lieutenant B 'Benjie' White, an Australian, had another such PRU Beaufighter. Together they started to supply Hugh Pughe with daily photos of whatever he wanted, whether in Sicily or North Africa. Soon, however, White was shot up on landing back at Luqa.

A feature of this operation was that the two highly modified PR Beaus also had 'modified' aircrews. The only other occupants of the aircraft being airmen ground photographers! They performed so well, and took part in so many close calls, that both were awarded the DFM. As neither man had any flying brevet or other aircrew insignia on their tunics, their DFM ribbons resulted in several arguments with the military police who tried to apprehend them for illegal display of awards. In the end Leading Aircraftman Ron Hadden and Corporal Norman Shirley only wore their ribbons when in known surroundings.

Both men recall that they came back with Warby over a dozen times with their aircraft damaged by enemy aircraft or by AA fire. Even more miraculous was that during February and March 1942, when almost every other aircraft on Luqa was destroyed or damaged on the ground, Warby's special PR Beau – T4705 – remained operational AND he was apt to park it insolently in the open opposite the underground Ops Room shelter, on those occasions when, after a morning sortie, he was planning to take-off again in the afternoon.

Eventually, after another 50 or so extremely valuable but dangerous ops, even T4705 became non-operational. Warby then managed to fly it back to Egypt with both Shirley (injured) and Hadden on board. Warby by then – March 1942 – had collected two DFCs and his first DSO.

* * *

The April 1942 super-blitz reduced 69 Squadron to virtually nothing and for a time Hugh Pughe was denied the intelligence he needed. Like manna from heaven, a PR Spitfire arrived, en route for the Middle East. It was flown by a young New Zealand pilot, Harry Coldbeck, who was merely delivering it and had no PR training. Within hours the Spitfire had been 'borrowed' and Harry found himself in the Squadron and doing PR work! Two Sergeant Pilots, Dally and Les Colquhoun, soon found themselves in the same situation. They too were ferrying PR Spits to the Cairo area but were waylaid.

Harry went on to become a flight lieutenant DFC and during the next few months flew in the region of 125 PR flights before being shot down into the Med but happily survived to become a prisoner. Les Colquhoun was later commissioned and he also became one of Malta's heroic pilots, receiving the DFC and DFM (and after the war the George Medal as a top Vickers test pilot). Malta had ways of making or breaking people. Harry and Les were among those who responded nobly when put to the supreme test.

After the May '42 battles, 69 Squadron rapidly built up its strength again. As well as the Spitfire Flight under Harry Coldbeck, it acquired a Baltimore Flight for longer range sorties and ship attacks, some more Beaufighters, some special Wellingtons with ASV for night searches and night torpedo attack, and even one or two of the Beauforts with which the unit was supposed to have been equipped months earlier.

Warburton returned again to Malta in August, at the height of the air/sea battles surrounding the 'Pedestal' operation[2], in order to keep an expert and watchful eye on the main Italian naval bases.

[2] This was a convoy, code name Operation Pedestal, essential to Malta's survival. It included the tanker *Ohio* which arrived much damaged. Only four other ships of the 14 merchantmen arrived, largely also damaged. The other nine were sunk en-route to the island.

He took over the Spitfire Flight from Coldbeck. This time he arrived from the Middle East in a PR Spitfire – one which had earlier been allowed to proceed beyond Malta! Although he was now a Squadron Leader, with instructions to limit his personal number of operations, he carried on much as before.

As the number of Spitfires increased and 69 became larger and larger, with Warburton now an acting Wing Commander, it was decided to give the PR Spitfire Flight its own squadron identity. Thus 683 Squadron was created with Warby in command.

No 69 Squadron was by then concentrating on not just finding enemy shipping but also attacking it in conjunction with Beaus and Baltimores or by night with torpedo carrying Wellingtons – 'Fishingtons'! Flying Officer Harry Donkersley, was part of 69 Squadron at the time and he successfully torpedoed several tankers and merchant ships at night in Fishingtons, thereby earning himself a DFC and bar in quick succession. One of his kills was the 2,552 ton tanker *Luisiano* which he torpedoed on 27 October 1942, Flying Officer W H Matthews sinking the *MV Ethiopia* with a cargo of aviation fuel, of the same convoy: this also with a Fishington.

Warburton's incredible luck deserted him momentarily when he was shot down over Tunisia by a 109 a few days after the Anglo-American landings to seize Algeria and occupy all French North West Africa. He managed to crash land at Bone, an airfield which had only been liberated by British paratroops just a few hours before. The place was many miles in advance of the army. Within five days, Warburton had contacted the French Admiral Villeneuve, Governor of the Province, persuaded him to throw in his lot with the Allied invading force, and then got the man to fly him to Algiers in a French mailplane. Once in Algiers he persuaded a Czech Halifax crew to fly him over to Gibraltar where he was promptly arrested as a possible spy due to his habit of flying in an unofficial uniform which included the carriage of knives and a German revolver ('They will never take me alive if I have to bale out!'). Eventually his identity was established, whereupon he borrowed a Fighter Command Spitfire, flew back to Bone and collected his camera and photo magazines. (Warby prided himself that he always brought back his pictures no matter what the opposition!) Refuelled, he headed for Malta and over the very spot where he had been brought down by the Me 109s, he encountered two Ju 88s. One he shot down but his guns jammed before he could get the other.

Arriving back on Malta where no news of these adventures had been received, and where he had become 'missing, presumed killed', he simply walked into the photo lab, tossed them the magazines and said: 'Sorry I'm so late with these.' Malta rejoiced; they thought their hero was dead.

* * *

If 69 Squadron was dominated by the rare accomplishments of Adrian Warburton, who by 1944 had two DSOs, three DFCs and an American DFC, all earned from Luqa, it also contained many other notable personalities. The example had been set by Tich Whiteley and the unit improvised brilliantly, especially when short of aircraft. For four years it existed at Luqa under an almost non-stop rain of bombs yet never ceased to operate effectively.

Few, if any, squadrons operated so many varied types in WWII, and few Squadrons achieved more. Its crews won almost countless DFCs and DFMs. It was also a multi-national outfit, and for a brief period, until shot down, 69 Squadron even had a French Tunisian Flight Sergeant, one who had daringly escaped to Malta in a float-plane.

Regardless of the hostile environment in which it had to exist, 69 Squadron kept Malta continuously informed. That information helped to keep Malta alive and be a constant thorn in the flesh of the Axis. To anyone who was there, the names of 69 Squadron, Warburton and Luqa were practically synonymous.

CHAPTER SIX

THE POOR BLOODIED BLENHEIMS

The Bristol Blenheim twin engined light bombers played an important role in Malta's fight against the Axis forces. However, there was a distinct 'Charge of the Light Brigade' aura attached to it. The expression – 'Poor Bloodied (or Bloody) Blenheims' – comes readily to mind. Apart from the early waylaying of the two Blenheims by 69 Squadron, the Blenheim story begins when it was decided to send a few Blenheims to Malta to see whether they could operate effectively from there. They came from 2 Group of Bomber Command, and their Senior Air Staff Officer at the time was Group Captain H P Lloyd MC DFC.

The half dozen Blenheims from 21 Squadron which flew out on this trial were led by Squadron Leader L V E 'Attie' Atkinson, a pilot who had earned a tremendous reputation during shipping strikes off the German and Dutch coasts. Not many lived to earn such a reputation as the casualty rate on such sorties was running at an appalling 30%!

Atkinson took the Blenheims to Malta in April 1941 – a long, tiring flight via Gibraltar. They were horrified at the conditions on the island compared to the purpose built airfields and building of their 2 Group bases and they had to have their aircraft serviced by the Navy. They flew a few raids, lost one aircraft in an air raid, but returned to the UK with a report that it was feasible to operate from the island.

As a result, two important decisions were made: one was that various Blenheim squadrons from 2 Group should take it in turns to spend a nominal two months or so on Malta; the second was that Hugh Pughe Lloyd would be promoted direct to Air Vice Marshal and sent to the island as AOC (Air Officer Commanding).

Atkinson was now a Wing Commander and commanding 82 Squadron, so it was natural that his unit be the first to fly to Malta, and so in early June, 82 picked up some tropicalised Blenheims and headed for the Mediterranean. It had been thought that the loss rate would not be so great operating from the island – how little did they know! Like many self-induced rumours in the war, the belief was that Italian sailors and gunners had little stomach for a fight and would quickly dive overboard when attacked!

Despite arriving in the dark and during an air raid, 82 Squadron was immediately put to work. On 22 June, two days after landing, they mounted a full scale attack against ships heading for Tripoli; the main Axis port on the North African coast. Both merchant ships and their destroyer escort threw up a hail of flak as the aircraft approached at low level. The result was devastating. Almost every Blenheim was hit. Flight Lieutenant T J Watkins had a leg almost severed and his navigator, Sergeant J S Sargent had to fly the bomber back to Malta under instruction from the badly wounded pilot. The CR42 which also attacked them was shot down by the air gunner, Sergeant E F Chandler. Getting back to the island, Watkins insisted on getting back to the controls, took over and landed, before passing out. He received the DSO, his crew got DFMs.

Squadron Leader J Harrison-Broadly's Blenheim was also badly hit but he carried on and completed his attack with one engine on fire, but then had to ditch. He and his crew were rescued and taken prisoner, but he received the DFC for his bravery. The two merchant ships were badly damaged but with the aid of tugs, eventually struggled into Tripoli.

Eric Chandler recalls this attack, not far from the island of Lampedusa

> It was soon made very clear that, despite hugging the sea, we had been sighted. Black puffs of smoke could be observed and after an interval, which seemed like ages, the sea both ahead and to each side of us started to erupt, as heavy shells hit the water. The formation, still closely following its leader, were turning first to the left, then to the right, slightly rising and falling. It was fascinating to see how the ships' gunners were constantly changing their direction of fire to follow our direction of flight.
>
> At this stage the leading vic of three turned to port while we turned to starboard. Out of the corner of my eye I saw the leading aircraft of the other vic, start to smoke from one engine, then the other. A sharp jolt to our own machine not only indicated that we also had been hit but threw me violently against the side of my turret. An unbelievable pain paralysed my right arm. I ducked down to check the arm, quite expecting to find it had been blown off! As I did so, a snaking line of Bofors tracer played across the aircraft,

passing through the perspex cover of my turret. This brought me to life with a vengeance and a determination to fight back.

I was amazed to find that we appeared to be flying just below deck level between two destroyers. Everyone on board these vessels were firing weapons of one kind or another and I at once opened up with my two Brownings in reply. Climbing suddenly, we clawed our way up and along the deck of the larger of the merchantmen, releasing our four eleven second delayed bombs as we struggled to clear the superstructure and funnels. Expecting we would then dive away and make for the open sea, I was horrified to find that we were still climbing and making a very clear target for the ships' gunners.

The reason for this was that our pilot had been wounded by a shell, which had torn away the calf of his right leg almost severing the leg from the knee downwards. To add to this, a machine-gun bullet had hit him between the legs. Our observer rushed back to his aid, pushing the control column forward to stop our rate of climb before we stalled. At last out of range we had a quick conference as a tourniquet was applied to the pilot's leg and it was decided to make for the nearest friendly landfall – Malta. We would try to make it before the pilot bled to death or the engines, which were now making very unhealthy noises, packed up.

It was at this point that my radio exploded into my lap and I observed a CR42 curving in for a second attack. I took my time lining up my sights, allowing the necessary deflection, and opened fire at almost the precise moment that he recommenced firing at us. At once his nose went up, then he seemed to slide down, tail first, then turning over, slid into the sea below.

Almost an hour later we were back over Malta. Wheels down, we motored straight in, cutting the engines as we touched the ground. One tyre must have been damaged for we started to swerve at once, ending in a ground spin. Getting out quickly I shouted for help then, scrambling onto the wing, I commenced pulling up and out our wounded pilot; while the observer pushed up from the cockpit.

Help arrived and I recall seeing Atkinson, Doc Monroe and Hugh Pughe Lloyd. We must have looked an awful sight. The observer was covered in blood, the pilot also very bloody but looking as white as a sheet, while I was thick with sweat, dust and dirt. The pilot was awarded the DSO – in my view it should have been a VC. He recovered but never flew operationally again.

No 82 Squadron had to be relieved well under the estimated two months, yet it had been an exceptionally quiet time. Before they were relieved by 110 Squadron, Atkinson carried out a daring and successful raid upon the main Sicilian harbour of Palermo early in July where a convoy was sheltering. He achieved complete surprise by first flying west, around Sicily, to approach the target from the north. After successfully hitting several ships he led the Blenheims fast and low over Sicily. For once all aircraft returned safely. They were credited with two large ships burnt out, another with a broken back, three damaged while a fourth was discovered being towed back to Naples.

The second squadron did not stay long on the island and before July was out, 105 Squadron arrived, led by Wing Commander Hughie Edwards VC. It is not a simple matter of saying that one squadron replaced another, for in practice, the shattered remnants of the departing one would be incorporated into the arriving one. A patched up Blenheim would join the new unit and patched-up crews would also be used to replace the lost crews. In effect there was just a Blenheim Squadron at Luqa. In any event, sound aircraft were never allowed to leave – Lloyd saw to that – and the crews returned to the UK by submarine or Sunderland.

There was no time for familiarization flights from Malta. There was neither the time nor the fuel. H P Lloyd had targets aplenty and no sooner were the new men on the island than they were being briefed for an attack. In the AOC's eyes aircraft were on Malta for just one purpose – to hit the enemy. If there were no ships to go for, then they would be sent to bomb other land targets. It was no use having aircraft sitting on the ground where they were in danger of being bombed.

To many, Lloyd appeared ruthless and at least two strong minded squadron commanders clashed vigorously with him. It was almost impossible to be more aggressively minded that Hugh Pughe Lloyd.

All the Squadrons went through various COs at alarming rates. During their short periods, 105 were commanded by Hughie Edwards (who left), and Wing Commander D W Scivier AFC (who was killed in a collision near Benghazi); 107 had Wing Commanders

F A Harte (a South African, missing 9 October), E S Barnes DFC and J S Dunlevie. 139 Squadron lost Wing Commander N E W Pepper (whose aircraft was blown up by exploding bombs from a first wave as he attacked a convoy on 3 June), while 110 lost Wing Commander T M Hunt DFC to an Italian fighter on 18 July.

* * *

Most attacks were made in dazzling bright sunshine which gave no chance of either a stealthy stalk or use of cloud cover. Although the Blenheims would approach at the lowest possible altitude to escape any radar detection that might be available to the enemy, they would be detected visually at considerable range and had to fly the last few miles in the knowledge that all element of surprise had been lost. Even at an early stage, when just smudges of smoke were the convoys's only indication, 'big bricks' from the escorts' larger guns would be thrown at them, erupting in great fountains of water as they headed in.

The more deadly threat was when the aircraft came within range of the Oerliken and Bofors type guns. Even with a maximum boost of 9lbs being used and airspeed showing up to 220 knots, those last few miles seemed never ending. By then the smoke smudges had turned into a forest of masts, then to the outlines of the ships themselves. As the splashes grew more numerous, the composition of the convoy could be made out and a fat target, such as a tanker, would be selected. Thereafter it was just a matter of jinking and skidding to try and avoid the gunfire; hugging the wave tops and praying.

If one survived the attack and got away, even the return to Malta was fraught with danger. A raid might be in progress and you may not be able to land having to stand off until the All Clear. With enemy aircraft about in any event, a Blenheim crew ran the risk of being spotted by an eagle eyed Me 109 pilot. Malta was certainly a most exciting place in wartime and every day the men survived seemed like a bonus. No place else was it easier to feel positively alive.

Successes were considerable, if costly. Up to 100,000 tons of Axis shipping was sunk by the several Blenheim squadrons, as well as raids upon land targets. A great one was carried out by the remnants of 18 and 107 Squadrons in early January 1942. The target was the enemy's main transport aircraft airfield at Castel Vetrano, attacked in daylight with the destruction of dozens of aircraft. The raid was well led by Squadron Leader George Lerwill DFC of 18 Squadron. A record number of ten serviceable Blenheims had been assembled during a lull in the air raids due to bad weather. More miraculous was that all ten got back!

Heroes were numerous – perhaps Ivor Broom is one who stands out. Originally with 105 Squadron, Sergeant Pilot Broom then joined 107 Squadron and found himself, after having carried out a number of successful attacks, one of the three senior pilots of the Squadron. As all officer pilots had been killed, Hugh Pughe promptly commissioned him in November 1941 and gave him the Flight to lead[1]. Before Ivor left the island, he had carried out 31 sucessful operations. Today, Air Marshal Sir Ivor Broom KCB, CBE DSO DFC AFC has readily affirmed – 'Malta changed my life...'

Ivor is one who regards Hugh Pughe Lloyd as one of the greatest of all RAF wartime leaders. It would also seem that Lloyd was a wonderful judge of character. Over and over again he would pluck an unknown from nowhere to find himself another 'ace'.

Another Sergeant Pilot who achieved fame was Ron Gillman. Not only did he also carry out a large number of successful attacks but he went on, in post-war days, to become a renowned civil pilot. He wrote a wonderful account about what it was like to fly Blenheims from Malta – the 'Shiphunters'. Ron Weeks was a Wireless Operator/Air Gunner who often flew with Gillman. He describes one action vividly

> We set course to attack two MVs escorted by a destroyer... the destroyer opened up accurate fire from three miles range... the sea was churned up by machine-gun fire and AA... No 4, 'Hoppy' (Sgt W A Hopkinson), went in and must have been hit because he hit the mast and blew up. We, in 5, had no time to swerve and had to fly through the flames of No 4. No 6 came after us and 'Grif had an explosive shell through the turret which knocked his tin hat over his eyes and went out the other side. He was jolly lucky. One MV sustained a direct hit from 'Gilly' and was left low in the water.

It is no surprise that Ron Gillman ended up with the DFM – and later a DFC. Ron Weeks, too, was commissioned and also received the DFC.

---

[1] When commissioned in Malta, Ivor moved into a room occupied by the author's brilliant ground radar expert, Al Glazer. Al greeted him with: 'You are my third room mate this week. I hope that you are going to last longer than the other two!'

A pilot who was shanghaied to join 107 Squadron was Australian Len Williamson. He was grabbed by Hugh Pughe en route to Egypt as soon as it was learnt that he was both a Blenheim pilot and an officer! The ADC's choice was again a wonderful one as Len was soon covering himself with glory. Also he kept a most meticulous diary. Sadly Len died a few years ago, but his diary remains. He noted each raid as 'Opus I, Opus II' and so on. This describes his fifth operation

Opus V. 13 December, 1941. Attack on shipping, Argostoli, Cephalonia. Six aircraft led by Pilot Officer Broom in two vics of three aircraft. Pulled up sharply to climb over the masts... dropped my bombs. Everything was very peaceful until I was over the ship, then hell broke loose. It seemed as if everyone was bent on shooting at little me. The destroyers and shore batteries opened up with machine gun, pom-pom and heavy stuff. Dived steeply for the deck and as I did so both motors cut out and Arthur was thrown upwards with all his navigation gear with the force of the move. The motors came on and I started to breath again. Kicked on hard rudder and kept throwing the kite around as hard as I could. The tracer was cutting across my path, yellow and red lines of it and black puffs were bursting around. Had on full power and kept hard on the deck as I pulled up over the hill at the end of the harbour. Pushed her over the top and was out of the line of fire of the guns. Just breathing a sigh of relief and grinned across to Arthur when Harry reported a Macchi diving down on us. Kept the taps open and concentrated on catching the leader. Line of machine gun bullets kicked up the water on my right and in front.

Harry kept me informed as to its whereabouts. Caught up the leader who had slowed down slightly and formated tightly on him. Macchi made about three attacks but the boys put a few bursts across his bows and he sheered off to have a crack at the formation coming after us. The leader reported a lone Blenheim behind us so he turned the flight around and went back to help him. All settled in together and continued towards home. Harry dropped his bombshell by telling me the turret had been U/S since we took off; could not rotate it, only depress and elevate it! He certainly learned his lesson.

Sighted the other squadron going in high up. Spotted a 'bogie' but it did not come near to us. The other kites had wireless trouble so we got the QDM.[2] Came into the island, circled and landed. We lost two machines – those of Sergeants Lee and Gracey – out of the second formation. The other squadron lost one but the crew got out.

His next sortie – Opus VI – was an attack on the coast road west of Zuara, Tripolitania, flying Blenheim 'Q' – Z7619, after aircraft 'W' had a duff wireless

Briefed to fly at 11.30 with Sergeant Ray Noseda as leader. Very overcast with occasional showers and I was finding it hard to keep my eyes open as I'd been up late the night before. When nearing the coast, spotted a plane high up but it didn't pay any attention to us; we closed up just the same. Noseda and I broke off from the main body and I fell in about a hundred yards behind. He pulled up over the sand dunes and as he did so disturbed a flock of ducks which flew into the air straight in front of my plane. No time to dodge and the next thing I knew we'd smashed into them. The impact was so great that the nose of the navigator's section was stove in and the heavy bodies of the dead ducks were forced into the aircraft. Arthur was hit in the face by one and just fell forward; blood, guts and feathers filled the cockpit and were kept moving by the fierce slipstream entering the nose.

The kite was very hard to control at this stage, especially as I couldn't see for the blood on the windscreen. The right wing dropped and it was all I could do to keep the kite from diving into the palm trees. Regained control – evidently there had been some obstruction in the right aileron.

Managed to keep Noseda in sight as most of the feathers and mess had blown to the rear. Couldn't get any sense out of Arthur as he was still dazed by the blow he'd received. Aircraft felt OK except for the drag created by the hole in the front so I kept on after the leader. Passed over some Arabs standing by a well and a camel nearby and I kept wondering if I'd be in closer contact with them in the very near future. Suddenly we spotted a train over to the right.

[2] A QDM is a radio homing bearing to guide the sender to the W/T station.

'L' immediately turned into it, attacked but overshot. I was too late to release the first time so came around again and, releasing my bombs early, let them roll along the sand into the train which had now stopped, blowing up the middle.

The occupants began pouring out and ran in all directions. Steep turned and came back firing the front gun into their midst. Too low to take good aim so sprayed with tracer. Dropped the other bombs and could see them bouncing towards the train, however, they bounced a trifle too high and went over the top and into a group of buildings on the side of the line where a lot of passengers had taken shelter and up they went. Noseda had scored more hits on the train and half of it was on its side and the remainder burning. 'L' set course for home and I opened up to catch him. Noticed some smoke to the east where our other planes had spotted a convoy to the north of us.

Tallyho came through and a line of bullets swept across the bow. Opened up to 9 boost and threw the old kite around as well as I could but the added drag made us sluggish, a CR42 was stuck dead on our tail and the bullets were whistling around us. I ducked instinctively as one explosive bullet hit the top of the cockpit and the little pieces of metal from it spattered Arthur's hand. Harry put a few bursts into him with no result but we were taking more than we gave out. Caught up with Noseda and formated. The CR2 made several attacks but our combined fire wasn't to his liking and after ten minutes he broke off.

Arthur held up his hand to show me and he was a sorry sight with a face caked with dry blood. Harry came through on the intercom to say that oil was running out of the port engine – it certainly was and the wing was one lake of it. Climbed to 5,000 feet in case the engine cut out.

The wireless had been put out of action by some bullets and the IFF aerial broken when we clocked the ducks. The weather was too thick up high and I had to keep close to the leader. It was raining when we came over Malta. I fired a Very and did a rapid low circuit and landed. As we taxied in, Arthur sat on top looking like a butcher's shop with a dead duck in each hand. There were five of the ducks which were comparatively whole and Harry and Arthur took them to their mess that night and had them cooked!'

Now came the attack on Castel Vetrano aerodrome, Sicily, as mentioned earlier. This for Len was his Opus XIII, Sunday, 4 January, 1942, led by Squadron Leader George Lerwill DFC

At Ops at 1.30 pm, learnt that all kites we could muster – ten – were to go and paste a 'drome in daylight, as it was overloaded with large transports and bombers, and a possible attempt to invade us was in the offing, especially in view of the unceasing raids we'd been having. I was to fly where I could fit in so chose No 4 in the starboard vic, which put me well in the middle to my satisfaction.

Bus down to the kites but had to wait beside them as there was no lull in the raids. All clear went so into the kites and got away in smart style. Kites all over the place but we finally sorted ourselves out and settled into formation. Difficult to maintain station as I was behind too many slipstreams and was being blown all over the sky.

When the coast came in sight we hugged the water and increased the speed. Swept over the shore missing telephone wires, buildings etc – very hard to concentrate on formating and looking out for obstacles in the way as well. Leader was weaving a lot and I nearly clocked a chimney at one stage. Rounded a hill and into a valley, passed over another town then stooged up a new valley. Pulled up over a hill and on the plateau lay the airfield. Released our bombs and they straddled the 'drome which was covered in aircraft, in the middle of being serviced. There were chaps running about all over the place.

The leader must have increased speed somewhat because his bombs were exploding beneath our formation which was a little behind. Felt a violent jar and my eye was attracted to the starboard motor by a flame. Looked rather grim but was only the exhaust stub blown off; the flame was being blown at us instead of the rear.

Opened right up and did violent evasive action. Last out too, despite all my vows never to get into that position. Caught up the formation over the sea. Everyone seemed to be OK but our formation dropped back and white smoke was coming from the port motor of the leader. Tried to call him up but couldn't raise him. Was becoming dark and I wasn't feeling too happy, not having done any night flying in these kites.

Arrived at Malta just on dusk so did a rapid circuit and landed right behind another chap, who cut me off. Few words of Arabic hurled at him too. Made an awful landing as I had to swing to the left to avoid him when he took his time getting off the runway. Our leader had been shot in the leg and his kite was holed a few times but the results next day, when photos were taken, showed 44 kites burnt out on the 'drome so we were very pleased.

Len Williamson rose to be an Air Commodore in the RAAF. His diary is perhaps, the best personal record of what it was like to be operating Blenheims from Malta at a time when the Luftwaffe in Sicily was active and on top.

With the return of the Luftwaffe, the plight of the poor bloodied Blenheim crews became more impossible than before. By February '42, losses in the air were still rising and planes on the ground were also being rapidly written off. Health and fitness became a problem too.

The final Blenheim squadron on the island was 21, which arrived three days after Christmas. It didn't last long.

It flew its first operation on 10 January, it's last on 22nd February. It lost eight aircraft in its last week, including its CO, Wing Commander W R Selkirk. One of the pilots was Pilot Officer Jack Booth who kept a diary of events. To quote from it

14 January 1942. Duke-Smith, Cameron, Oakley and self. Low level shipping sweep off Kirkennah Islands. Duke-Smith leads; I am No 2. We sight 5,000 ton MV escorted on our side by a destroyer. Flight Lieutenant Duke-Smith leads us round to the west and we attack. D-S hits a mast and is lost. I follow and drop 4 x 250lb bombs in a stick by pilot's bomb release tit, weave and escape. Oakley is shot down but Cameron gets through, joins me and we return to Malta. There is smoke from the ship and it is likely that all four aircraft released their bombs at zero feet. We claim a 'believed sunk'. It certainly should be sunk.'

The CO and Jack make an attack against the African coast six days later

20 January. Low level trip over sand dunes on North African coast near Horns. Bomb buildings which look like stores and then proceed along coastal road shooting up a lorry convoy before returning unscathed. White and Dagnall make similar trip to Zugra but both machines hit.

White and Jack Booth made a low level sweep off Horns on the 26th but saw nothing so they flew inland, bombing and machine-gunning lines of petrol bowsers

26 January. These low level raids to North Africa were reasonably safe, exciting and fun. We never know what to expect as we came in from the sea, except that the coastal road was bound to turn up eventually but the road might be empty or with a convoy handy as on this day. We rarely met with a fighter escort and usually only spent 10–15 minutes on the road. The gunner, Sergeant Andrews, had a wonderful time.

27 January. Low level shipping sweep off the Kerkenna Islands. Within sight of a MV and escorting destroyer we were attacked by CR42 fighters and turn back. Aircraft holed in fuselage – also other aircraft. No losses.

29 January. Low level attack on German HQ west of Tripoli but made a bad landfall so bomb coastal road. Flight Lieutenant Fox hit by exploding bombs of Selkirk and crashes – others OK.

Jack Booth was made acting flight commander following the loss of Flight Lieutenant E Fox. Then on 4 February, after a couple of tries, six aircraft set out to attack the harbour of Palermo, Sicily, led by the CO, with Pilot Officer F J Workman, Sergeant M Houston, Booth and Sergeants Dagnall and J Ibbotson.

4 February. We set out in two vics of three, the CO leading the first and myself the second. The track was westerly around the toe of Sicily, then north, out of sight of land and then turned into the coast from the west. We were at zero feet and once past Pantelleria we had no land or wind check – dead reckoning.

Excitement – the coast near Palermo sighted on the horizon but as we drew nearer my New Zealand navigator –'Monty' de Malmanche – noted that we were too far south and that the CO should be turning left towards the target. So I held my vic back so that we could cross behind the CO as he turned and be on his starboard – but he held course.

We were within sight of a beach and small town when the CO hit the sea. There was much debate later as to whether he was hit or misjudged his height but in any event he had gone. His wingmen – Workman and Houston, pressed inland and we followed well behind. Now, of course, we were not going up the valley behind Palermo as planned but into a cul-de-sac of high hills with the upper parts covered in cloud.

We dropped our bombs on a road bridge behind a small town and in view of the low cloud I decided to take my vic up through the cloud as the safe route. Full throttle and up through 10/10ths cloud into sunshine. Not a sign of another plane so we circled for a time but eventually set course for Malta.

The cloud disappeared near the coast and we reduced height to sea level without incident. Arrived back to find that Dagnall had already landed and we were the only two to get home. Knowing our lack of instrument flying, I suspect that all those missing after the loss of the CO, flew into the hills in cloud as they were not practised in blind flying. It could, of course, have been that they were shot down – in any event, we never knew.

6 February. Low level attack on shipping at Bueray. Mitchell returns with mechanical trouble. Remainder believed shot down by 109s off the coast.

11 February. Another sweep off Kirkenna Islands – nothing sighted. Sergeant Stubbs shot down off Malta by 109s.

13 February. Three out of four Blenheims arrive from Gibraltar – one is shot down off the coast.

19 February. Various sweeps off African coast. Bomb transport and roads.

22 February. Dagnall – solo trip to attack Palermo. We learn the best news of all time – we are to leave this God forsaken piece of rock tomorrow!

After this last Blenheim squadron had been almost decimated in a week, it was, decided that Malta was not the place for this now almost obsolete bomber to operate. It had had its successes but quite a few people considered then, and now, that the price paid was a heavy one. So the poor Bloodied Blenheims departed, defeated but not unbowed.

If emphasis has been given to the diaries of Len Williamson and Jack Booth, due credit must also go to many other heroes. Attie Atkinson, who led the successful attack upon shipping right into Palermo harbour destroying three ships and damaging as many again; Pilot Officer Buckley, Wing Commanders Pepper and Harte; Flight Lieutenant Edmunds, Flying Officer Allport, to name but a few.

Many were decorated. Flight Lieutenant Watkins received an immediate DSO, but sadly, many were also killed, although few attacked as often or in a more determined manner than Ivor Broom. When by December 1941, these attacks had forced the enemy to abandon the short route to Tripoli and to use instead the much longer one via the Greek coast, devastating attacks were launched upon the harbour at Navarino Bay and that of Argostoli: devastating for both sides, unfortunately. Another Blenheim triumph was to cripple the *Reichenfels*, the newest and largest of the enemy supply ships, on her maiden voyage.

Sergeant Pilots figured largely in most operations, often leading vics of three aircraft. Crossley, Kidby, Noseda, Crowe, Hamlyn and others carried heavy burdens on their young shoulders. The few who lived to tell the tale rapidly acquired manhood but supplies to Rommel were much curtailed and, as the epilogue of this book records, the results sent ripples, much to the Allies advantage, which spread to all theatres of the European War.

CHAPTER SEVEN

HOW THE OTHER HALF LIVED
(AIRMAN KEN ROGERS' DIARY)

It's a lovely day! The sun is high and hot, hardly a cloud in sight and the water in Birzebuggia Bay is crystal clear. Walking along the shore road, you can see right down through the water, to the rocks on the bottom.

The blue Mediterranean – it really is true. Across the bay, shimmering gently in the mid-day heat is Kalafrana, our seaplane base and workshop area.

Not too long ago, if you had enough money, you could have holidayed here – Malta – this tiny jewel in the blue sea. I suppose we are lucky the war had brought us here and we are being paid for it – no posting to frozen Russia or battling up and down the dusty desert with Rommel in hot pursuit. No, this is what I volunteered for, because the Battle of Britain was over and life on a Spitfire OTU was too far from the war; this is lovely.

If only those blasted Germans and Italians would leave us alone, if only for a few hours, we could enjoy our 'sceptred' isle. No – there they go again, the sirens wailing and being taken up all over the island, till their mournful warnings fill the air – the air, where daily our war is being fought. With the same ingredients that the Battle of Britain had contained, only this time, we are over a thousand miles from Britain.

A tiny beleaguered garrison, with hardly any supplies, hardly any planes, hardly any fuel, hardly anything in fact! Living day to day and hoping we won't become another Crete.

I continue my walk along the shore road, only now a little more warily. The peace of the day has been broken again, there is mischief afoot, or ahigh might be a better expression, because the big Naval, land based guns are already banging fiercely away. High in the sky the shells are bursting and now you can see the – Ju 88's this time – quite a number of them, seem to be heading our way. Maybe it will be Luqa – or our own station Hal Far, about a mile up the road – or perhaps a slight turn to the left and Kalafrana will be on the list.

Not to worry, they are not overhead.

These are the opening paragraphs of a diary written and kept by Leading Aircraftman Ken Rogers during his time on Malta between March and August 1942. To many who served on Malta it was by far the worst period.

It was the non-stop bombing which dominated everyone's thoughts. Then, following the 'Glorious 10th of May', although the bombing was still a menace, day and night causing death and destruction, it was the shortage of food and almost everything else that people require for civilised daily existence, which became predominant. Even water, during the hot months which followed, was in short supply.

Fortunately for history, Ken Rogers – humble 'erk' – was there to record it all: the bombing, the daily grind in almost impossible circumstances; the lack of virtually everything to keep the aircraft flying, while existing on a near starvation diet. Moreover, he records it all with British tolerance, fortitude and humour.

The diary covers many thousands of words – far too long, unfortunately, to record in full within these humble pages. But we can delve into it and read and try to understand what he and his companions went through. For those of us who were on Malta it has an all too familiar ring. For those who can only imagine what it was like, read – and learn.

It's a lovely day. The Spitfire guns and cannons are audible now, firing in short bursts mainly; they are in amongst the 88s, the formations are breaking up, some bombs are being jettisoned as the bombers turn and run. People are fighting for their lives up in that beautiful sky; an 88 is coming down in flames, another with an engine streaming smoke is trying to dive from the pursuing Spits – fights are going on everywhere and some parachutes are drifting down, hopefully all enemy ones.

The bombing attack is a shambles now; an 88 appears from the direction of Hal Far, no higher than a thousand feet, going like hell, right over my lovely bay, with a

Spitfire hanging on to his tail like a terrier, firing burst after burst into it. Not for long. The 88 loses height and disappears in an immense cloud of spray, into that blue Mediterranean. The Spit pulls up in a jubilant roll and circles the spot, while across the bay in Kalafrana, the engines of the Air Sea Rescue boat are throbbing as it noses and heads seawards, looking for trade.

I am conscious of another noise, as though of rain on the water and pattering on the road around me. The Bofors guns had, as usual, joined the Naval guns and the barrage of anti-aircraft fire had been intense. The spent pieces of shells are now returning and my tin helmet is a block and a half away, in our billet at 6 Pretty Bay – well – it had been such a lovely day and I was only out for a walk along to the cafe to see if Maria had any food under the counter. Too late now. Better nip along to the cafe and get out of it.

My decision to nip along, also comes too late, as there is a sudden blow on the top of my uncovered head. My God! I cover my head with my hands and run to the protection of the nearest doorway. A gentle probing reveals a piece of anti-aircraft shell – quite small – strange – it felt like half a shell hitting me. There appears to be little damage and only a slight bleeding. I have been lucky – it could have been a much bigger bit and my morning walk would have terminated. 'Not to worry' – our popular phrase gets used again, the metallic rain has ceased – I made off in the direction of the cafe.

Wonder if Maria has got any grub? Looks like you might survive after all. Put the bit of metal in the tobacco tin – souvenir – a true numbskull now!

It's a lovely day!

Everything seems to be back to normal, didn't see where the bombs fell after all. Probably a few more on Hal Far – shake the day shift up a bit. 'Here we are – 'Shem Maria' and 'Hallo' and 'How are you' (in my rather poor Maltese). She talks of the many air raids, to which I agree and something else which is beyond my vocabulary, so that's enough! Small talk over, let's get down to the main item – 'Big Eats Maria?' I ask. At this she looks sad and holds out her two hands in front of her and in Maltese informs me that

Big Eats are a thing of the past – finish – spitchered. Because of the war!

Ah well, it was only a hope – wonder if she has any beer? – try again – I ask for a beer! It's worked! She's getting a bloody beer.

It's a lovely day!

This was the life in spring and early summer 1942 – after the earlier struggles, first with the magnificent Gladiators, then the Hurricanes and anything else that could fly, valiantly fighting against the superior 109s and overwhelming odds, until the delivery of the Spitfires starting on March 7th. May 9th saw the delivery of the fourth batch of Spitfires.

It is very important to be able to fight back, because nothing is so soul destroying as to have to sit there and take it and not be able to retaliate. Especially when your homes and billets and all the other secure things in life are being systematically destroyed and people are getting killed and maimed, or being driven out of their minds by constant, unremitting air raids.

That is why quite a good number of us Hal Far boys came to be living in this lovely spot at Birzebuggia – Pretty Bay – and it is a pretty bay. Hal Far is flat – or nearly so – the stone peacetime billets have been flattened, the hangars have been flattened, sundry other buildings have been flattened – the enemy have been busy.

It hadn't been a very big aerodrome to start with but it was a nice one. Pens are springing up all over the airfields – Luqa, Ta Kali, Hal Far – as our good friends the army boys, together with our own lads and the Maltese labourers, are really getting them up. We even have the army lads helping to refuel our planes! This is life or death stuff – ours!

The guns are going again and the recipe seems to be the same as the last one – more Ju 88s, more bombs, more noise and more dust and smoke – only this time, it is more interesting because most of our gang are on the roof and the comments are good:

'Where are they bombing this time?'

You call that bombing?'

'Must be Luqa – hard luck lads.'

'Better them than us!'

'The Spits are amongst them.'

'Get at 'em lads.'

'There's one of the bastards going down.'

'Great stuff – the f — — — had it!'

'There's another flamer!'

'Serves the bastards right.'

'Shouldn't have joined if they can't take a joke.' And so on…

We are enjoying our enemy's downfall and excitement mounts as our Spits carve up the 88s and some 109s. We are counting now and also keeping track of the parachutes and we have our rifles handy in case one of the enemy planes comes near enough, and low enough, for us to have a shot at them; it's good for morale to be able to hit back, but no luck this time. It's a lovely day!

The raid is ending again and another parachute is heading for the bay – a tempting target but that wouldn't do – though we have heard stories from the pilots that enemy planes have been shooting at our lads in their parachutes.

The Air Sea Rescue launch is heading out from Kalafrana again – more trade – the sun is shining.

It's a lovely day!

There is another air raid before we leave for work – much more desultory this time – bombers are much higher and not very determined – must be the Italians – they break off the engagement before they reach the targets – we are worrying them now!

We also have another ace up our sleeves in 1942 – an ace in the shape of Group Captain Woodall – or 'Woody' as he is affectionately known. One of the most outstanding fighter controllers of the war, who had masterminded Tangmere and Duxford Wings as well as Douglas Bader and his warriors during the Battle of Britain. He is now doing his stuff again and our fighters are benefitting from his vast experience of fighter direction. It is still early days but there is a feeling about that we are winning a bit.

* * *

There is another problem. The bomb disposal Chief (who by now deserves a VC) has discovered that a 500lb unexploded bomb, in front of one of the pens housing a Spitfire we are going to work on, is due to go off in about 10 minutes – or so he thinks. The Spitfire is at risk; we will have to move it out of the pen, but quickly! 'Taxi it out!' is my immediate suggestion (I love taxying Spitfires) but this is immediately vetoed by the Chief, who says the vibration may set the bomb off. 'Better push it out,' he says. This is not too well received, as his time prophecies are not always accurate.

Our own Technical Chief solves the problem - 'Quick, everyone round it and push it round the back of the pen – you've got ten minutes!' We are off at the double with many and varied remarks being bandied back and forth. People's ancestries are questioned; trepidation is high. Someone leaps into the cockpit and releases the brakes, chocks are heaved out of the way; there is no need for exhortation on this job and the Spitfire is practically airborne by the time we pass over the top of the bomb, everyone pushing like mad, and round the back of the pen we go. There is now a solid stone wall between our precious plane and the bomb.

The brakes are barely applied when with an almighty bang, up goes our bomb and we are showered with dust and rubble. 'Chief Bombs' estimate was a little over generous, but not bad. Our Spitfire is safe – so are we. Within minutes the army boys are filling in the bomb crater and rolling it flat for us to put the Spit back in the pen. All's well again; the sun is shining. It's a lovely day.

Better get our evening meal before the cookhouse closes, so in we troop – feeling in our bags for our cups – mugs – tin can – mess tins – or anything that will hold the 'offering' and a cup of tea.

Culinary equipment is in short supply, as the cookhouse has it's quota of enemy attention too! We file past the serving table holding out our receptacles – one or two still have a battered enamel plate – most – mainly half a mess tin – the other half is for tea. The cook ladles in a spoon full of his latest 'Cordon Bleu' effort – which tonight is 'biscuit duff, flavoured with pilchards – or maybe that should be pilchard, singular. Oliver Twistwise I hold out my mess tin hopefully but he pushes it away with an empty spoon – 'That's your lot mate.' We collect our tea from the big urn and being extremely careful not to drop anything – find a corner in which to sit. From our bags, we produce our 'irons' as they are called – comprising knife, fork and spoon (should you still be fortunate enough to have them) and the remainder of our breakfast ration of bread.

The latest thing in Hal Far is to give each person at breakfast, their bread ration for the day. This situation was arrived at by virtue of the number of complaints from the lads, saying they were not receiving the proper ration of bread and this could have been true. The daily bread ration at this time for us, is 10 ounces, which, being rather brown, heavy bread, does not look much at all. To last for 24 hours, it means two thin slices for breakfast and two slices for the evening meal – if your outlook is optimistic! If, on the other hand, your outlook is pessimistic and you don't think Mr Hitler's lads will let you see the day out, you scoff the lot at breakfast time in case, (a) you get the chop, (b) your bag with the bread in gets bombed, or (c) someone nicks it!

Food generally is a problem. There is not a lot left on the island and rations are getting smaller and lacking in variety. Food in the cafes is now virtually non-existent, our own canteens have none, so we are entirely dependent on the rations from the cookhouse. Weights are dropping and thin men are becoming the norm, but we can run faster – a most useful asset when the enemy decides its your turn today.

We examine our evening meal – the biscuit duff avec pilchard is worth investigation – as biscuit duff avec anything now comprises our main diet. It started life as a flat, square, very hard, pale brown biscuit, manufactured by several UK firms but mainly, we suspect, by Spillers – the dog-food people. Not only that, it is said, they were made for the First World War and have been in storage since. This would account for their unique taste. One or two other estimates of their age have been made – the Crimean War and even the Napoleonic Wars have been mentioned.

Whatever date they were manufactured, we would be lost without them, as they are now the mainstay of our diet. Our cook soaks them in a huge vat of water, probably for weeks, and when they are soft and mushy, like mashed potato, he adds the flavour of the day. This varies according to the meal; tinned fish is suitable for breakfast or evening meal, some corned beef makes a tasty lunch, or even a stray Oxo cube. A little cocoa, and eureka, and we have a chocolate pud! We drink our tea – that blue, brown indeterminate liquid and wash down the last of the duff and bread, then we are ready for another few quick puffs before taking up our duties.

There is much speculation about the tea and it is frequently the subject of discussion. 'Holy Water', or even 'Maiden's Water' has been mentioned, and down the spectrum to 'pure and unadulterated gnat's piss' – which is probably an insult to a gnat. It also, it is said, contains this other magic substance – supposedly bromide – which is responsible for the bluey tinge and is added to help take away the airmen's evil and constant lust for women; to reduce his sexual longings and safeguard the local maidens.

On the rations we now receive, it is very debatable, whether anyone can sustain an onslaught on the local ladies – if they are indeed available and that also is debatable. As for the lads who are married locally, or have current girl friends, no statements are issued. We all – nevertheless – drink the stuff and care not – we are more interested in survival than theoretical orgies.

The sun is going down now – soon our little lights will be going on. Oh, no! There it goes again – sirens sounding in the nearby towns! We have our warning system on the aerodrome – this is a hand cranked shrill warning and is our own take cover signal – we take no notice of the normal sirens. It does, of course, sometimes happen that our own warning does not sound, until after the bombs have fallen – or the 109s have nipped smartly across the aerodrome at zero feet and either strafed or bombed us. This leads us to have slightly less faith in our own warning system, than perhaps we should have, and so we prefer to keep one eye on the anti-aircraft fire and shell bursts – they can tell us far more about who is going to get what – and when!

Tonight it seems – it is going to be our turn – the 88s are marching towards us and – oh yes – there goes our warning – a short one -the operator knows a better place to be. Three or four of us move to the rear of the pen, with an eye on the bombers, trying to see if they have dropped anything yet but it is dusk – nothing is visible – the 88s are, however, just about where they should be if they have dropped anything – 'F—- this,' says Taffy – 'We're going to get it.' Our ears are straining for the familiar whistle. Or worse the rushing sound – that means we are the target for tonight – when we are treated to a prolonged series of loud cracks, in all directions, like giant rip-raps going off – then comparative silence.

'What the F—- was that?' says Taffy. We look around – there is a strong reek of explosive but our Spitfire seems intact – as we are. Outside the pen, the aerodrome has a large number of small objects littered around – like a one pound tin of meat, with the tin split longitudinally and hinged upwards and the whole contents suspended from it. A new device for us this time – they are up to their tricks again.

Shearer meanwhile, has picked one up and after a brief examination, throws it across to another lad nearby – it explodes between them – luckily without harming either – their faces are a study – language is picturesque.

Chiefy 'Bombs' is now shouting – 'Don't touch them, they are antipersonnel bombs with a limited blast area – but dangerous close to.'

We need no second warning and now treat them with the respect they deserve – one has blown the crankcase off our army despatch rider's motor bike and he is annoyed. Miraculously, there is little damage to the planes but the aerodrome is littered with the A/Ps. 'What now, Chiefy?' We ask – the drome is U/S and our night fighting Hurricanes, will be taking off for Luqa shortly.

He has the solution, 'Rifles lads – pop 'em off!' Just the job, in no time, we are blasting off in all direction, with a curious mixture of armour piercing, ball and tracer ammunition, anything that has been left over from the machine gun belts out of the old Spits. The A/Ps are popping off in good style.

We are now more at risk from our own gun fire, than from the enemy action, luckily Chiefy has the matter in hand again and under his direction we line up and advance together, like a Hollywood epic. In a short space of time, we have exploded them and our aerodrome is serviceable again. Back to work lads, the fun's over!

There is now talk about this new hazard, on a small field like Hal Far, this A/P weapon could cause problems by it's saturation effect. Ah well, not to worry! Because of the war!

We are barely out of the cookhouse when the sirens go again, closely followed by our own 'take cover' warning. Four Me 109s, at high speed, low over the aerodrome, a quick burst of cannon fire and four bombs are down. But this time, two of our Spits are on the tails of the last two; one Spit puts in a burst, a good long one, and the 109 rears up, then plunges down towards Grand Harbour, smoke pouring from it. There is an audible crash and an ominous cloud of dust, flame and black smoke arises. One less German to worry about. There is great excitement and cheering at this grandstand performance, taking place as it did, practically overhead. We also bet the other Spit would be successful, as he was in an ideal position for an attack.

The 109s with bombs on are becoming a nuisance. We get little warning of these; they sneak in fast and low, sometimes our only warning is a burst of cannon fire, then the bomb. One of our armourers tells us the 109 bomb release is activated by pressing the firing button for the cannons. This seems to be true as the one usually precedes the other.

Not far away from our house, on Delimara Point, is situated an anti-aircraft battery, which is equipped with big guns; someone said they are Naval guns. Whatever they are, they are of a large calibre, and when they do blast off, everyone around here is aware of it; the muzzle flash is awe-inspiring, the noise deafening! The lads who operate them must have a job coping with it all. They cope very well and their shooting is accurate. High level stuff, up amongst the bombers. They can't do the high speed stuff like their cousins – the ballet dancing Bofors – but they have knocked a good few down.

The Bofors, on the other hand, fed by small magazines, rip the shells off quickly; they are good at the low level stuff. It is a joy to watch a well trained Bofors team during an action – there is hardly a pause in their guns pumping a stream of shells skywards. They too have built up a good score of aircraft destroyed. They have also, on several occasions, when the enemy was having his own way, become the target for the bombers and have suffered considerably. That must be a compliment; they are worrying the planes.

We have night fighters – Beaufighters and occasionally our Hurricanes, operating from Luqa, which has a long, permanent runway system and is more suitable for night operations. The Beaufighters with their airborne radar, are having good successes lately and have built up a score of enemy aircraft destroyed. They are hunting tonight and there is a small amount of enemy activity going on. One of the radio operators tells they have shot one down already.

One of the Beaus is being vectored on to an intruding enemy plane and has been given interception instructions from the ground controller – the pilot presently confirms he has a contact. One of our own lads tells us they are approaching the north west end of the island and we may be able to see the action. I nip back up the steps and intently search the dark area of the sky in question. There is not long to wait, there is a flash from the Beau's cannons, shortly followed by the noise of them and suddenly there is a glow, which rapidly develops into a huge sheet of flame falling earthwards – a 'flamer' – our lads have another victory. I dash back down in time to hear the jubilant pilot. 'An 88 – got the bastard – he's down in flames.'

Our Ops room staff are in fine spirits, that's the second victory and it seems there are still a few more enemy coming over from Sicily, nothing on a large scale but more of a nuisance value to disturb everyone's sleep.

We listen attentively, someone else has a vector and he is in hot pursuit, in roughly the same area. Perhaps another JU 88 – with it's German crew, full of food and drink, straining their eyes for the sight of our tiny island, then bomb doors open and down goes its contribution to our ultimate downfall. 'A quick about face and in no time at all, we will be back at base, eh, Hermann?' 'A Hermann,' the pilot of the 88 has it all worked out. 'Much better at night, eh, Hermann?' The Spitfires are no good in the dark!

Which is of course quite true – but unknown to them, our Beau is steadily gaining on them, guided by the radar operator in the rear seat. Hermann is shortly in for a nasty shock and I want to witness it. Back up the stairs and strain intently for another welcome sight, Hermann and his gang on the way down, the hard way.

But there is another noise, disturbing my concentration, getting louder, an aircraft engine, practically screaming and close, bloody close, what the hell? It can't be? Sounds like a STUKA, not here? Not at this time of night! This is no time for a personal arguement, I take-off, but quickly, heading for the Ops rooms steps, with that terrible rushing, screaming sound we have learned to dread, getting louder and louder. My feet are not moving quickly enough, the noise is beating me. I make the doorway and turning right, start to descend the stairs, when there is one almighty crunch and the blast heaves me down the rest of them and I arrive in a heap at the bottom.

Two Fleet Air Arm pilots pick me up and ask, 'What the hell was that?' 'Sounded like a Stuka,' I reply, 'But I didn't hang around to find out.'

One climbs the stairs and immediately shouts down, 'It's started a fire in the armoury.'

One of the lads seated then informs us, 'There is blasting powder in the bottom room, to demolish the hangar.' Chiefy Bomb, in his spare time is blowing up the dangerous bits of buildings and he has his explosive store in what is left of the barrack block, about 20 yards from the Ops room. The two Fleet Air Arm pilots are up the steps and I follow. We run towards the blaze caused by the bomb, 'Looks like an oil bomb.'[1] 'I head one way – there are, in fact, two fires – one close to the building wall and the other about ten feet away. Inside the door of the building are a couple of extinguishers and I grab one and hand the other to a Fleet Air Arm pilot. We each tackle a blaze and in

---

[1] The enemy attacked us with every kind of bomb in his armoury; small ones; medium ones; large ones and bloody big enormous ones. Incendiaries, anti-personnel bombs; delayed action ones. Bombs that burnt on contact and gave everyone near a bit of themselves. Bombs that dug in before going off; they were good as the blast went mostly upwards. Oil bombs and of course, he machine-gunned and strafed us with cannon and guns. Variety was indeed the spice of life!

no time my blaze, at the building wall, is quickly subdued, the other one is also dying rapidly, not a minute too soon. We hear the noise of another plane getting louder.

'Quick,' I hear, 'back down the Ops room!' The fires are out, no further reason for hanging about and the three of us beat a hasty retreat.

At the bottom of the steps one of the pilots, a youthful looking two-ringer asks, 'No bones broken after your tumble?'

I reply, 'Probably have a few bruises tomorrow.' To which he says, 'Well done!'

My bruises are forgotten, I feel ten feet tall.

* * *

June 12th. We hear a convoy has left Gibraltar and is coming our way. It has six merchantmen and a large escort with two aircraft carriers. We also hear another convoy has left Alexandria for Malta, on June 11th – supposedly a big one, but it is being heavily attacked. Wonder if they will make it?

It is June 15th before our Beaufighters can cover the convoy, by which time it has had a severe pounding from the bombers. We hear the Italian fleet is attacking them as well.

The Fleet Air Arm Albacores are attacking the Italian fleet and we hear they are withdrawing. The Wellingtons and Beauforts from Luqa are in action and finally our Spitfires get into the battle. It is a terrible time for the seamen trying to help us – the losses have been enormous. We now hear the Alexandria convoy has had such a bad time they have turned back! It's not worth it.

By the time the other convoy reaches us, only two merchant ships survive (the *Troilus* and *Orari*) – luckily they are big ones and have flour and anti-aircraft ammunition. The significance of their arrival is known to us all. Had these two ships been sunk as well, Malta would have fallen, for our stores were nearly at an end. The cool, clear, blue Mediterranean has a carpet of sunken ships, crashed aeroplanes and dead men, for miles and miles around Malta.

HMS Welshman, the minelaying cruiser, with a top speed of 40 knots, had left the convoy and made another solo dash, a thing she is famous for, and arrived here on the 15th. She had a cargo of new Spitfire engines, nearly 200 tons of ammunition for the cannon and guns, coolant for the engines and some mail. She also brought smoke generators to make smoke over the Harbour.

As June draws to a close, we begin to feel that perhaps we will not be invaded – not yet! The enemy is occupied elsewhere and hasn't the time or resources to waste on us. On the other hand, we are doing a lot of damage to the convoys carrying his supplies. Can he really afford to ignore us for too long? If he had possession of Malta, his future in the Mediterranean would be assured.

*   *   *

Poor Hal Far collects a few more scars – and I collect one or two as well. The day started pleasantly enough and we were working on our various tasks. Mid-morning there was an alert and on the way back to the dispersal from the flight office, two of us were confronted by a 109, heading towards us at about 50 feet! No discussion or second thoughts were necessary; as one we were off, heading towards a lorry, filled with stone blocks, parked close by. The guns of the 109 were firing but we were winning.

My companion went under the front of the lorry and myself slightly behind (must be losing my grip), shot my legs forward and in the same sliding movement, caught the side of the lorry with both hands and performed a nice, easy backslide under the lorry.

The firing continued for a moment or two, then the noise of the 109 faded; the danger had passed – we had beaten the rascal. It also dawned on me that my backside was sore. In my haste it had acted as a brake and the rough, stone strewn surface, had removed several square inches of my skin and there was a small wound in my left leg. We emerged and were aware of activity in a small group of airmen nearby. Two had been hit, one seriously, but in no time they were taken away in the ambulance.

The nearby sickbay applied some soothing ointment to my nether regions and removed a small piece of steel which had just pierced the skin of my leg. Nothing serious – lucky again.

July 14th, 1942. Air Vice Marshal Lloyd, who was our father figure at the helm, was posted. He had been in charge through the worst of the battle and was well liked. His successor is a famous commander who has seen plenty of action – Air Vice Marshal Keith Park. He knew his stuff and wasted no time making his presence known. He has an offensive spirit. Malta has to start giving it back – in quantity! He also wants the Germans shot down before they reach the island.

He often appears, unannounced, in his little MG Tourer with a Maltese driver, on the aerodromes and talks to everyone. He is a good man to follow Hugh Pughe. Morale is high. This man says we are going to win – guaranteed! The trouble is, we are not overstocked with aviation petrol, in fact, we don't have too much at all. It is doubtful if our planes can sustain a large scale offensive. Up to now we have been on the defensive. Getting petrol to Malta is becoming practically impossible.

The sun is high and hot, there is hardly a cloud in the sky and the weather is still crystal clear, it is barely 24 hours since I last enjoyed the beauty of our bay. There have been several air raids on our little jewel of an island in that space of time. A fairly average day for us and our enemy, it has been going on for some time and looks all set to continue, we are used to it.

We turn into our street and file into our house. Steve wonders if there will be any water on, it very often isn't. Right now, I would enjoy a good soak in a hot bath, remembering the long concrete bath, full of hot water we used to wallow in after our school rugby games, to help ease the bruises and soak the muck off. No such luck, but Steve triumphantly announces there is indeed a trickle of water. 'Fill the basin if you can,' shouts Taffy. We have no bath in the house – or shower, there is a small stone sink and one tap and a metal basin. If Steve can get a reasonable amount in the basin, we can get some each, in a mess tin or cup or whatever, this generally suffices for teeth and a shave and perhaps hands and face! If we are lucky and the water is on for a while, we can fill the basin individually, stand in it and have a complete wash down. We have no toothpaste and very little soap.

This morning we are lucky and Steve leads the rush – no point in going to bed dirty. I climb up and look around our lovely bay – it is peaceful and quiet and the sun is hot. These characters will be half an hour at least, so it's on with swimming trunks and a short pad to the water's edge and a lie back in the blue crystal clear Mediterranean. That helps, the cool water is a tonic. After about ten minutes of relaxation, it's up on a flat rock and lie back, this is magnificent. Our bodies are all burnt dark brown, except where our shorts normally are, we can soak up unlimited amounts of sun, what a life. It's another lovely day!

Back at the house, the Welshmen have completed their ablutions and are stretched out in bed, talk is running down and we are all tired. There is still water available and I wash off the salt and rub down and into bed myself, that's much better, even without a mattress – AAAH!

From Taffy – 'Hope that bloody siren doesn't go.'

From Steve – 'Hope those bloody fleas leave me alone.'

From Hughie – 'Shut up for Christ's sake – I'm tired.'

From myself – 'Wake me up in time for night shift.'

We sleep!

A day in the life of an airman, during early 1942, things could be better. We are intact – a lot are not!

After a suitable period, a few of us wander up to our flat roof, the sun is going down, it will be dark very shortly. To sit on the parapet of our flat roof, on a calm, warm evening and watch the sun slowly sink out of sight, until it's last rays light up the heavens and any odd clouds, is a moment to be appreciated. The war seems very distant, everything is too beautiful and peaceful to think of death and destruction. There is some music playing nearby, it takes you back in time,[2] to the happy times at home, listening to the orchestra my father played in and of your own small contribution. You

---

[2] Quite a number of our lads received only two or three days embarkation leave before being post overseas, some, in that short space of time, contrived to get married. After the usual period of time, they received news that they had become fathers. Some, who had been overseas for two or three years, had a child growing up they had never seen. One of the lads on Luqa in our squadron, after he had been overseas at least two years, had a letter from his wife, saying she had given birth to a son. He was delighted! When someone queried the length of time he had been away from home and asked did he not think it strange with the time lapse, the answer was received, 'Not at all, nothing strange about it, there was a gap of three years between the first two children!' Who were we to disillusion him?

remember the kaleidoscope of colour, as the dancers whirled round the ballrooms of your home town, of the warmth and friendliness of bars and the smoke rising from a good cigarette. You remember a lot of things best left forgotten.

Like a great big whacking meal!

The beauty and the loneliness of it all, can be overflowing at times, it is not a good thing, trips down memory lane, can have an unsettling influence. We are saved by an unfamiliar sound, an odd, splashy, puttering sound out in the bay. We are immediately alert and on the lookout, six pairs of eyes strain to pierce the gloom, then suddenly we see it, a submarine moving into our bay, this invokes comment.

'What the hell's it doing here?' 'Where's it going?'

' Is it one of ours?' – Good question!

'Maybe it's come to take us away.'

We make our way to the bottom of the street, where there is a small jetty, which juts out into the bay and has a pipeline running along it, our submarine makes for it.

We haven't seen a sub in Marsa Scirocco before and we are very curious as to the reason for this visit. In due course, some of the seamen come ashore and we greet them, some have time to spare and we take them under our wing, we have little to offer them in the way of hospitality, but they have obviously been made aware of the conditions here. We have plenty to talk about and they have proper fags, which they offer around freely. Some of them are heavily bearded, all are enthusiastic about life in subs, they commiserate about our food and the bombs, for my part, I wouldn't exchange jobs!

Submarines have, for some time now, been playing a very useful role, in carrying supplies to Malta, several have been engaged in this very dangerous task and have had a lot of their very essential equipment taken out, to make way for cargo. They have brought essential medical stores and mail, clothing and paraffin, and most important of all, they have been bringing aviation fuel. Some of the fuel comes in the submarine tanks but a lot is carried in the 4 gallon tins, in wooden crates, lashed on the outside of the sub, to the casings.

What this must do to the trim of the submarine and how it must affect it's diving capabilities, must be a headache to them. What it must do the safety of the sub, is almost beyond consideration. Aviation fuel is highly volatile, the 4 gallon tins are made of wafer thin metal, like a large biscuit tin, they are also famous for leaking. Our worthy seamen are living in a floating bomb and for about three weeks at a time, the smell of fuel alone must be sickening. They admit the storing trips, as they call them, are not over popular, carrying the cargo they do, offensive action is not possible and some are spending a lot of time on the surface. They mostly come from Alexandria but one or two, we hear, have come from Gibraltar and an odd one or two from the UK.

If they did but know it, the seamen are playing a very important part in our married men's morale as they bring a good quantity of mail, half of it is probably Steve's.

They cannot stay long, as the sub must leave quickly, no one hangs about longer than necessary in Malta nowadays. Before they go, to our delight, they give us a tin of 'Ticklers' or Navy fag tobacco and some 'Rizla' fag papers, we cannot thank them enough, we are rich men.

They promise to call and see us, if they are in the vicinity again and bring more stuff next time. That would be most welcome, we assure them and wish them luck in their travels, in a very short space of time, our friends have puttered off into the night. 'Ships that pass.'

We make a start of smoking ourselves to death. There is a lot of clandestine activity around Malta at night, in our bay, we have regular visits from flying boats, mostly operated by BOAC and carrying no armament. They carry passengers, vital spares and mail, etc. They are crewed by merchant airmen, who are flying long and dangerous journeys to various parts of the world.

During the long nights, the flying boats are normally turned round and flown out again the same night. In the short summer night however, it sometimes happens, that a flying boat would be hidden in a hanger at Kalafrana, during the day. The enemy has knocked off quite a few that were left at a mooring in the bay.

Luqa too, has it's share of nightly visitors: Whitleys, Hudsons and CW20s land and unload and in turn take back mail, passengers and air crews who have finished their tours. They shuttle between Malta and Gibraltar and also the Middle East.

We are not completely isolated.

We talk far into the night about our visitors and, thanks to their generosity, we are enjoying our first good smoke in ages. We talk about the subs.

'Fancy having good fags all the time.' – Hughie

And lots of jam in the mess.' – Taffy

'And good bread and butter.' – Steve

'And tins of fruit and cream.' – Self

'And a lovely big depth charge up your arse!' – Taffy

For all the comment, we would not swop jobs.

The next decision to be made is, how soon do we smoke the 'Ticklers'? Where did it get it's name from?

The trick, when rolling the fags with loose tobacco is not to make them too tight, or they won't draw and not to make them too loose, or the tobacco all goes down your throat, at the first puff. We know the drill!

One of our Spits landed away from the pens on an exposed dispersal near the cliffs. The engine had a small fault and the pilot switched off when he came to a halt. I went over to work on it and noted that it practically pointed in the direction the low flying, bullet spraying 109s usually came from. I took off the brakes and pushed the tail round until it was in the right direction. Back in the cockpit, with the reflector sight on for a moment to check the elevation, and the stage was set. If those little pigs came over while my job was under way, and they crossed my path at the right height and range, the firing button was going to be pressed – if I was quick enough. If – probably one chance in a million of hitting anything, but it made me feel better. Needless to say nothing did appear, which was just as well as Chief would have roasted me – unless I had hit one!

We go into August, fully aware that we are not working too hard. The Spits have got less and enemy action seems to have lost its enthusiasm. By the 5th or 6th, Chief gives us the news that another convoy has left the Clyde – a big one. He mentions 14 merchantmen and a huge escort. This time it must be a peak effort. To help them in their passage, Middle East is lending us planes to carry out attacks on the enemy airfields. Being mostly bombers they will be based at Luqa and will require extra ground staff to look after them.

The next day we rattle off in a truck for Luqa. Not unusually, no one seems to know what we are doing there! By mid-afternoon some of the pieces are falling into place and we have a billet in a big, sprawling, building that in peacetime used to be the Poorhouse.

Luqa, by comparison to Hal Far, is a big aerodrome with a hard surface and runways. There seems to be a good number of aircraft around. We see Beauforts, Beaufighters, Wellingtons, Spitfires, Baltimores – there is much more action here and we look like finding employment.

We make the acquaintance of Flight Sergeant 'Nobby' Clarke, who has a ginger moustache but not a lot of hair left. He is at least 50 and his peacetime job was selling insurance. 'Are any of you engine fitters?' he asks us. Two of us are, Taffy Newton and me. Nobby beams and utters, what we soon discover is his most popular phrase – 'You're trapped!' Grand, we want to be trapped.

He writes down Taffy's details and asks him if he has any experience of Wellingtons. Being honest, Taffy says, 'Fuck all, Chief, I'm a Spitfire expert!' Nobby's smile barely alters as he quickly says, 'Good show, you've got 24 hours to become a Wellington expert.' Taffy has been trapped!

Chief now turns to me and he notes I'm an ex-Halton Apprentice. 'Any Wellington experience?' he asks. 'Sorry Chief,' I reply, 'but if they have Bristol Peggies in them, we took them on our course. Won't take long to put the rest together.' Nobby is pleased. We are off to a good start – ex-Brats[3] have a place in his heart.

When he has taken the names of the other lads, he proceeds to tell us that the 'Wimpies' are going to knock seven bells of shit out of the enemy aerodromes over the next few days. This sounds like a good idea and we are here to help with those arriving from the Middle East. Meanwhile, he suggests we go and look over some of his resident 'Wimps' with a view to familiarisation.

Our Middle East friends will be with us in the early hours of the morning. Two riggers and myself are allotted a pen, well up in Safi Strip, and when our aircraft arrives we are to give it a good inspection. It has to be ready by the next

[3] Affectionate nick-name for ex-Halton apprentices.

The Author, post-war in uniform of BOAC Captain

Harry Colbeck, 69 Squadron. This New Zealander was waylaid with his Spitfire in Malta. He proved himself an outstanding PR pilot.

A unique photograph of the three Gladiators in Malta. The island lived on 'Faith' and 'Hope' but, as can be seen, it was hard to discern 'Charity'. Taken in June 1940 before the hangars were demolished. *Jim Pickering*

Squadron Leader P B Lucas DFC, OC 249 Squadron, Malta. 'Laddies' many contributions included his knack of getting the best out of the controversial 'ace' George 'Screwball' Beurling. *D Langois*

Wing Commander A Warburton – Malta's greatest Ace and Christina of Malta with visiting American sailors who had gallantly helped to bring in one of the few surviving ships of the August convoy by serving as ships gunners. Whilst serving at Luqa he was awarded two DSO's and four DFC's. *Imperial War Museum*

Authors crew in Cairo. Left to right: Sgt Lightowler (co-pilot), F Sgt Laird (Beaty's navigator), F Sgt Evans (Wireless Operator), Sgt Haynes (kneeling), F Sgt Evans (wireless operator/air gunner), Unknown, W O Wavell (navigator). *D Haynes*

One of the watches from the Malta 'Ops' room. *Marian Gould*

Some of the author's Malta crew relax in Cairo along with other tour expired SDF crews. Left to right: Unknown, F Sgt Evans (Wireless Operator), Unknown, Sgt D Haynes (wireless operator/air gunner), Sgt Lightowler (co-pilot), F Sgt Laird (Beaty's navigator). *D Haynes*

night even if we have to work on it all day. We locate the pen but find no amenities. No hut, no oil stocks, no hot or cold running water, just a big empty pen. Things are tough on the strip! We make sure there are no old bits of metal, shrapnel, or anything likely to damage the tyres of our aircraft, lying about in the vicinity.

It is in the wee small hours that Wimps are in the circuit – perhaps one of them is ours. We have two torch wands to greet them when finally we see and are impressed by the sight of our Wimp, navigation lights on, its pilot gingerly feeling his way up the track in the dark. I wave the wands and get an answering flash from the landing lamp and he follows my directions until we reach the pen.

We are blessed with a good pilot. At the pen mouth I spin him round with a minimum of fuss, signal shut off engines and put the torches out. After shouting 'brakes on', the crew begin to emerge with an assortment of bags and full of cheer. One hero hands us some sandwiches from their night flying rations they had not consumed. We are rich men! The pilot, last to emerge, is a tall flight lieutenant. I bid him welcome and ask if the aircraft has any snags. We are lucky again, things are quite good it seems, apart from a small mag. drop on the starboard engine. A truck appears and the crew disappears into the night.

We start work. It is slightly downhill into the pen, so with the help of the lads in the next one we push our Wimpy back into the safety of the stone wall – just in case. It is very doubtful that enemy aircraft will visit our island, as they will be busy attacking the convoy, although we still have no firm news of it. The sandwiches are shared out and we have an unexpected feast – 'desert chicken', bully beef, really, but it tastes like fillet steak.

The sky is lightening. Jock, one of the riggers, and I set to work on our inspection. 'Glum', (he looks it), the other rigger, puts the wheel covers on to stop the oil drips from the engine from fouling the tyres. He makes a life's work of it. The amazing thing is, in the middle of our efforts to do our small best towards winning our war here, you still come across people who are not very interested in doing anything to help, as long as they can get away with it. Glum is not alone. Not to worry – Jock will have his foot up his arse before the day's out, or I will miss my guess.

With the aircraft fully serviceable, I report to Nobby, and also ask him if there are any spare plugs. He says yes and taking some, I retrace my steps to the pen. I find Jock hopping mad. He had discovered the hydraulic system needed topping up and told Glum to do it. Our silent friend had then proceeded to pour half a gallon of hydraulic fluid down the Very Light exit tube; all over the wireless set. He had mistaken it for the opening to the hydraulic reservoir – or so he said!

His life was in danger from Jock, from the wireless mechanic, who was now feverishly working on the radio, and from me, as I had told Nobby our plane was ready. Jock told him to get out of his f — — — sight and keep out, as we started to mop up the damage. Half an hour later, our wireless mechanic pronounced the set in working order and we were now shipshape again.

Late in the day our crew returns, rested and refreshed. They are all quite incredulous about conditions here and food in particular. Wonder if they got the same tea? The skipper is sorry he didn't bring any more grub with him, and fags, and soap – you name it. So are we! The skipper says they are going for the enemy aerodromes – Cagliari is one of them, which will be a help to the convoy battle. Not long afterwards the Wimp trundles off towards the runway. It will be several hours before they return and we go to Nobby's office.

* * *

Time drags on. Finally a phone call from Ops informs us that the planes are returning. Thankfully Jock and I make our way up the strip again. We don't have long to wait until our bold boy appears with the minimum of fuss. Our crew is jubilant. They have plastered their target, starting fires and destroying planes on the ground. The skipper has no complaints about the aircraft. Jock and I snug the Wellington down for the night; we will give her a good check over tomorrow.

News is that the aircraft carrier *Eagle* managed to fly off some Spitfire reinforcements before she was sunk and we have also received a batch from *Furious*, so things are looking good for the fighter squadrons. If only we can get in some good ships and a tanker.

Can you imagine being on a big, unwieldy slow moving tanker, with fuel oil and aviation spirit in the tanks, being subjected to a continuous series of attacks from sea and from the air, knowing that one good hit will put you in a blasting, roaring, conflagration that will roast you in seconds, or blow you into a flaming sea. How much pay would you give these people, or what kind of medal do they deserve? I know my answer!

Suddenly there are Swordfish on our side of the 'drome, taxying in and coming to a halt near our squad. Surely they are not going out on a daylight strike, against the Axis might, these venerable biplanes, with a top speed of next to nothing with a torpedo on? The leading seaman air-gunner, in the nearest one, assures us that this is so! They are going to attack the Italian fleet he reckons. We suddenly feel great sympathy for these lads. What chance have they got against such superior forces?

In no time they lumber into the air, and seem to take ages to disappear. We are still hanging around when they return – those who survived – shot to pieces. Our leading seaman air-gunner is carefully lifted from his rear cockpit. He is alive but in a sad state; he manages a grin. What kind of medals do they deserve?

Once the Wellingtons return to Middle East we are unemployed. Our gang of four wanders about and finally comes to a halt at a pen with a blue Spitfire in it – with no guns, and a couple of lads working on it. We discover it is one of Squadron Leader Warburton's planes. He is the photographic ace and is in the process of building up a flight and is short of men. We see the Chief and get the job.

I am paired with a bluff, stocky Lancashire lad, rigger – Jack Meadows. Being Lancashire myself, we have plenty to talk about. Jack brings me up to date on some of Warburton's and 69 Squadron's exploits. We also check out a Spitfire and shortly the pilot appears. Jack greets him affably, pulls his leg and calls him Les. He introduces me. This is Les Colquhoun. We strap him in and in no time he is off in a cloud of dust.

Prior to Warburton's return from a spell in the Middle East, Flight Lieutenant Harry Coldbeck had been running the Flight. Not long afterwards the great man – Warburton himself – appears. From Jack's description I had expected a dashing, blood and guts type, but here was much more gentle type; well mannered and soft spoken. I take an immediate liking to him.

The next morning we are awake early. There is a lot of action on the aerodrome. This is a vital day, our Spitfires will be able to give a lot of support now the convoy is nearer. According to the latest information, three merchantmen should make it today, a further one is still afloat but in trouble, and the vital tanker has had such a beating it is doubtful if she will make it. The tanker is essential for our survival, so a constant stream of Spitfires are making an all out effort. Beaufighters are battling away as well.

It is shortly after 6.00 pm when the three merchantmen arrive in Grand Harbour. *Port Chalmers, Rochester Castle* and *Melbourne Star*, battered and blistered. The local inhabitants cheer themselves hoarse. Meanwhile our fighters are still in the battle. The tanker *Ohio* is still afloat. We spend the evening in a wave of renewed optimism – our future looks much better; if only the *Ohio* can make it.

The following day brings more hope. About mid-day the *Brisbane Star*, with a big hole blown in her bows, arrived in the harbour – a magnificent feat. *Ohio* is still afloat – just. Little do we know what an epic struggle the gallant tanker has put up. Against all the odds she beats the sea and the might of the enemy. With a destroyer lashed on one side of her and a tug front and rear, she enters Grand Harbour at 9.30 am on the 15 August. She is a grand ruin, but her precious cargo is safe – we can continue with our fight.[4]

[4] A complete copy of this wonderful 'diary' has been lodged with the Imperial War Museum in London, by Admiral of the Fleet Lord Lewin KG GCB LVO DSC.

CHAPTER EIGHT

THE EQUALLY BLOODIED BEAUFORTS

It is doubtful whether the crews of the Blenheims or the Beauforts had a shorter expectation of life when operating out of Malta. What is certain is that neither could reasonably expect to live over long. It was indeed rare for either crews to survive more than a month or two of anti-shipping operations without being shot down; or at least having their aircraft shot up with fellow crew members killed or wounded.

The Beaufort crews were probably the more vulnerable, even if their aircraft was able to withstand being hit somewhat better. Due to the necessity of having to drop their torpedoes under controlled conditions, the Beauforts were the more obvious 'sitting ducks' to the efficient gunners aboard both the ships being attacked and their well-armed escorts. The Blenheims could, and did, attack at maximum speed; swiftly diving down from a number of different angles – very much according to the individual's personal theory of how best he could put his bombs on target and still 'get away with it'. Whereas the Beaufort pilots knew that their torpedoes would be unlikely to run true unless the aircraft speed was approximately 140 knots; unless the wings were held level, not just for the drop but also for a second or two thereafter; unless also the aircraft's attitude was more or less dead flat and unless their 'fish' could be dropped at a range of 600–800 yards from its target, at a height of 80 feet and with the aircraft more or less 60 degrees from the ship's bows, allowing for the ship's speed to meet it. All this with a barrage of flak splashing all around them and with no instrument other than the human eye with which to gauge the range and with only the pressure altimeter, which at best, gave a hazy idea of the aircraft's height above the featureless, often dazzling, sea.

The best hope for either type was to achieve a surprise attack. This could be achieved in several ways – at least in theory. An attack in the dark or in the half light of dawn or twilight was known to be effective but the problem in these conditions was to find the convoy and then position the aircraft correctly so that the several required parameters of height, speed, range and angles of attack could be attained. In theory also, an attack against a background of a mottled countryside (shoreline) was also liable to catch the sailors by surprise but such conditions were unlikely to be found unless the ships were hugging a coast. By far the best hope of achieving surprise would be to make a run with a low sun behind the aircraft. It was also possible to attack from out of a low cloud bank but, here again the problem was to find ships in these weather conditions; not to mention cloud, in the sunny Mediterranean!

A few Beauforts of 217 Squadron were fitted with an early type of airborne radar (ASV) but the sets were elementary. However, these aircraft were better able to locate convoys under adverse conditions even if the range scale was in miles rather than yards and therefore almost useless for accurately providing an exact distance from which to drop the torpedo.

To survive a series of operations against hostile convoys in Beauforts based on Malta, it was almost necessary to be blessed with a big measure of luck. To achieve success, the pilots also had to possess an almost unlimited measure of courage – fortunately a quality that was not lacking.

Many attacks, whether by Blenheim or Beauforts, were made by small formations of aircraft – often flying in vics of three planes. Since the leaders of these formations were usually officers, often flight commanders or even squadron commanders, and since the leader tended to become the most obvious target for the ship's gunners, the chances of an officer surviving was, if possible, even less than that of a sergeant pilot captain. One result of this, as we saw in the Blenheim chapter, was that these units, after a short spell of ops, were almost all dominated by young NCO pilots. Several squadrons were so decimated that Hugh Pughe Lloyd, and later Keith Park, quite often gave reliable sergeants immediate commissions, followed almost at once by a rapid jump to flight commander.

* * *

Malta in 1940–43 was the place where, in quick time, the proverbial sheep were sorted from the more determined goats. It made men or it broke them. The bombing was incessant and the operations were, at times, almost suicidal. No matter what the cost, supplies had to be stopped before Rommel, already by the summer of 1942 poised at El Alamein, could take his last thrusting steps into Alexandria and

Cairo. Above all else Axis tankers had to be stopped. By 1942 there was precious few of them left in the Mediterranean.

Fifteen Beauforts of 217 Squadron arrived in Malta – spread over two days (10/11 June '42). They had flown out from the UK in the usual two stages. First a flight from an airfield in Cornwall to Gibraltar, then by the more dangerous Gib to Malta stage. True to form, one was attacked and damaged during this second stage by a marauding Me 109 and arrived with a dead gunner on board. It was to be the first of many casualties!

The Beauforts had been sent to the island for two specific purposes. The immediate one was to attack the Italian fleet which was menacing a convoy to Malta. Second, and equally demanding, was to stop Rommel's supply ships. Rommel had already routed the British 8th Army and had advanced far into Egypt. He stood at a then insignificant and unknown town and railway station at El Alamein, just 60 miles from Alexandria where the British Eastern Mediterranean fleet lay at anchor. For the first time since that see-saw Desert war had commenced almost two years earlier under the Italians, Rommel and his Afrika Korps had seized a port not too far distant from his front line. Tobruk had fallen.

The Germans and their Italian ally were swift to take advantage of this capture. Not only did it give Rommel a port reasonably close to his front line (in earlier battles Tobruk had been surrounded but not captured) but it also enabled the Axis forces to bring supplies to that port without coming within range of Malta's only torpedo carrying aircraft; the FAA's old Swordfish and Albacores on Hal Far aerodrome.

Axis convoys now passed eastward through the Straits of Messina or departed from bases such as Taranto and headed immediately East until reaching the coasts of Greece, Corfu or Cephalonia. Then they turned south to Tobruk. These convoys had to be stopped if Cairo and Alexandria were to be saved. The torpedo carrying Beauforts were now to complement the efforts of the Navy submarines, and other forces ranged against the convoys.

But first there was a more immediate and urgent task. Malta was being starved to death. Not only was it short of food – down to its 'last crusts of bread', but desperately short of fuel, ammunition, fresh AA gun barrels, and so on. Unless a good sized convoy could get through the island would very soon be starved into surrender.

This would have been a major tragedy since, a month earlier, the Spitfires had wrested air superiority from the Luftwaffe during those glorious May air battles over the island.

Desperate measures were being attempted to relieve the beleaguered island. Convoys code named Harpoon and Vigorous were being simultaneously attempted. The former would sail from Gibraltar, the latter from Alexandria. Even if one convoy were to be slaughtered, then perhaps the other might escape some attention!

Under normal circumstances the Italian Navy did not over exert itself to attack these well defended convoys. The British Navy, although having fewer, smaller, slower and less modern ships, had managed to beat off and defeat all earlier attempts to reach these convoys. However, circumstances had changed. A very few brave and determined Italians, literally riding astride ingenious one man torpedoes, had penetrated the anchorage at Alexandria and immobilised both British battleships there. As a result the eleven merchantmen which set forth from Alex, were escorted by nothing larger than cruisers and destroyers – although *HMS Centurian* was dressed up to look like a battleship in an attempt to fool the enemy.

The enemy was not fooled. As the supply ships proceeded towards Malta so did a large Italian battle fleet sally forth from Taranto to intercept. Even before they left the UK, 217 Squadron had been alerted to this situation; so it seems probable that Ultra intercepts had alerted the British to this fact. 217's immediate task once on Malta, was to halt that battle fleet before it could inflict mortal damage on Operation Vigorous.

Air reconnaissance was so often the saving grace of Malta. 69 Squadron was, as usual, keeping Air Vice Marshal Lloyd fully in the picture. On 14 June, an aircraft from 69 detected the Italian battlefleet as it left port. Hugh Pughe – not for the first time – came himself to Luqa to brief the new arrivals. His pep-talk was, as usual, dramatic and demanding. He had the ability to inspire his audiences with a genuine 'do or die' fervour.

The evidence was that the Italian fleet was proceeding in two sections. One comprised the two mighty 35,000 ton modern battleships the *Littorio* and the *Vittorio Veneto*, with a screen of destroyers. Ahead of this was a cruiser squadron of four fast and powerful ships as well as a protective destroyer screen.

The attack upon them was planned to take place at first light. This required 217 Squadron's Beauforts to take-off in the dark. Nine aircraft became available, led by their CO, Wing Commander W A L Davis.

There now occurred one of those strange incidents which often help to change the course of history. One aircraft found its passage from its dispersal pen to the runway blocked. By the time this could be cleared, the others had all departed. Henceforth, the Beaufort, flown by young Flying Officer Arthur Aldridge, was on its own.

Mass torpedo attack was the best chance of survival – also the best way of ensuring at least one hit. Once running, the torpedo leaves a 'give away' trail of air bubbles as they track towards their target and many a ship has avoided destruction by being able swiftly to turn away from the telltale track. It is known as 'feathering' the torpedo. But if half a dozen or more torpedoes are dropped more or less simultaneously and from different directions, then the chances of a ship avoided them all are less favourable. It also tends to divide the defensive gunfire amongst the attackers. But for a lone aircraft to attack a battlefleet in daylight at the required 140 knots on a steadily held course – this was akin to suicide. Not only is the flak concentrated, but a lone torpedo run can be avoided. Yet Arthur Aldridge pressed on anyway – in hope.

Wing Commander Davis does not seem immediately to have found the enemy fleet. All flights from Malta tended to suffer from an almost total absence of reliable meteorological data. It was anyone's guess what the wind vectors might be over the featureless sea, 100 miles or so away. Also the Italian's course and speed could only be estimated – at best an inspired guess. As a result, although he had departed after the others, it so happened that Aldridge was the first to detect the enemy ships. He came upon the advanced cruiser squadron – four cruisers protected by eight destroyers. Although he had to circle around to get into a favourable attacking position, not one shot came his way.

It was early dawn but the visibility was more than sufficient for lookouts. Wisely, Aldridge instructed his gunners not to fire at the enemy while he carefully continued his run into position and successfully launched his 'fish'. It was only then that a fusillade of gunfire came at them but by then he was skilfully jinking and skidding his Beaufort towards safety.

The torpedo ran true and the 10,000 ton cruiser *Trento* was well and truly struck. Smoke began to pour from it and it was brought to a halt. Destroyers rushed to its aid and soon had it covered by a smoke screen. While it burned, Arthur Aldridge and his jubilant crew were winging their way to safety back to Malta. As it happens, his aircraft had been spotted by the Italian lookouts but it was the first time the Italians in the area had seen a Beaufort and it was not immediately regarded as hostile. Also, his half circuit of the fleet had fooled them into thinking it was a friendly reconnaissance aeroplane which had arrived with the dawn to help protect the fleet. Not until it was too late was it recognised as British.

Soon thereafter, Davis and the other seven Beauforts arrived. Such a group was obviously hostile and they were met by a barrage of anti-aircraft fire. The Beaufort formation split itself into two sections. Three attempted to torpedo the battleships while the other five concentrated upon the vanguard of cruisers. One, at least, had a go at the smoke enveloped *Trento* without realising it had been brought to a halt already. As a result, using the customary 'aim ahead' tactic, the torpedo passed harmlessly in front of the burning ship.

Sadly all the torpedoes of the main group appear to have missed. Most were probably dropped at too great a distance from the big ships. Few of the crews had ever tackled so large a target, so distance could be difficult to judge, especially with the intense gunfire coming at them. Perhaps it was significant that Aldridge had previously had some experience against a battleship while in England. He had been in on the Channel Dash fiasco (12 February, 1942) and had dropped a torpedo at the *Scharnhorst*.

The *Trento* may have been saved but lurking beneath the waves was the British submarine *HMS Ultra*, whose captain found himself unexpectedly in the middle of a milling crowd of Italian ships as they tried to avoid the torpedo attack. Bravely remaining at periscope depth, the submarine took advantage of the confusion to fire a salvo of torpedoes into the stricken cruiser, sending it, and most of her crew, to the bottom.

Not long afterwards, RAF recce planes were able to report that the fleet had turned tail and were heading back to Taranto. Whether this was a direct result of Aldridge's and the sub's attack is not known, although events further south may have been an influence. There, the ships of Operation Vigorous were taking a beating from Luftwaffe Ju 87 and Ju 88 dive bombers. The merchantmen *Aagtekirk* and *Buthan* were sunk. Worse still, the cruiser *Hermoine* and the destroyers *Hasty, Airedale* and *Nestor* had also gone down. In addition, the dummy battleship *Centurion* and three other cruisers had been damaged. It was at this point that the remaining ships had turned back towards Alexandria.

Perhaps the greatest outcome of the successful destruction of a major Italian warship, was that never again did an Italian battleship put to sea against the Allies. Were it to have done so two months later, in August against the Pedestal convoy, then it is almost certain Malta would have been lost.

Meantime, Operation Harpoon had fared a little better. As the convoy neared Malta they too came under attack from the deadly dive bombers. It was a smaller convoy – just six merchantmen, plus escorts. Four were sunk but the *Orari* and *Troilus* got through. *Orari* was damaged but a total of 25,000 tons of desperately needed food, arms and fuel was unloaded from the two ships. This enabled Malta to keep going for about another eight weeks. This time had been bought at a terrible cost, for the escorts had lost the destroyers *Kujawiak* and *Beduin*, while two cruisers and three destroyers were damaged.

As can be seen, dive bombing was far more effective than torpedo attack, a fact brought out in the Pacific War with the Japanese. However, neither the RAF nor FAA had an effective dive bomber at this stage of the war, so torpedo attack it had to be: or low level stuff in a Blenheim.

There was a second Beaufort unit in evidence during this battle, No 39 Squadron, based at Sidi Barrani, headed out soon after dawn on 15 June. Their orders were to find the fleet, attack, and then carry on to Malta. They were escorted by Beaufighters of 272 Squadron, while B24 Liberators of the RAF and USAAC were to bomb the ships from high level. Two hours later, off Derna, the twelve Beauforts ran into Me 109s of 8/JG 53, long before the ships were found. Two Beauforts were shot down and five others headed back damaged – one crash landing behind the Axis lines, its crew being captured. The remaining five, led by Wing Commander A J Mason, the CO, and a Flight Commander, the determined Squadron Leader R P M Gibbs, pressed on, guided by a 69 Squadron Maryland from Malta. The five Beaufort crews also seem to have been misled by the sheer size of the battleships for they too dropped their 'fish' too far away. Most of the aircraft were hit by return gunfire or suffered damage from the 109s, but none were lost, although two, including the one flown by Gibbs, had to crash land at Luqa. 39 Squadron did claim two hits but this is not confirmed.

The Liberators did slightly better. One hit the *Littorio* with a bomb without seriously impeding it. One Lib was shot down by a 109 pilot from JG27, 60 miles out to sea. Two Beaufighters were also lost to the 109 fighters, one by each to JG27 and JG53.

Following this emergency, 217 had orders to proceed to Ceylon, but Hugh Pughe had other ideas. He was never a man to let a useful attack unit slip through his fingers. 217 remained on the island; as also did the survivors from 39 Squadron.

Attacks were successfully made on a number of Axis ships but the losses mounted alarmingly. Flying Officer F Minster was shot down by a flight of Ju 88 fighters from I/NJG 2 on June 20, and the day following, three of 217 were lost while attacking a convoy which included the valuable, large, new freighter, the *Reichenfels*. Other Beauforts and their crews were hit – Flying Officer Aldridge being wounded – but the freighter, loaded with 241 vehicles and over 4,000 tons of fuel and ammunition – both desperately needed by Rommel, was eventually sunk.

Soon after this 217 and 39 – or what was left of them – were amalgamated into what was then known as the Malta Beaufort Squadron, and Pat Gibbs, promoted to Wing Commander, put in charge. Later a few Beauforts from 86 Squadron were also incorporated into the new unit. Crews were being lost on almost every strike but successes were also made. Among the vital enemy supply ships which were hit and generally sunk, were the *Rosolino Pilo*, the fuel carrying MVs *Istria, Delphi*, and the *San Andrea*, which alone carried nearly 4,000 tons of fuel for the Afrika Korps.

Gibbs led one attack on 23 June, and although two Beauforts went down with three others, including his, damaged, they claimed hits on the two merchantships which had to go into Taranto and transfer their cargo to other ships. On 3 July these ships sailed, being found off the Greek coast, at the extreme end of the Beaufort's range. Gibbs led the attack, which damaged one ship, but two Beauforts were damaged, Gibbs again being one, forcing him into another crash landing on Luqa.

He continued leading sortie after sortie, scoring hits and sinking ships. Success came on 21 July off Cephalonia. On 20 and 21

August he attacked the 7,800 ton tanker *Pozarica*, damaging it on the second attempt. It was later seen beached off Corfu.

The final nail in Rommel's oil coffin came on 30 August, after the 5,000 ton tanker *San Andrea* was found. Escorted by Beaufighters, Gibbs came at the tanker from the land, having crossed the Italian coast so as to attack from the side least expected. Despite Macchi fighters he put his torpedo into the side of the tanker from 500 yards. Moments later it exploded while the other Beauforts were still making their approach. Gibbs got the DSO for that, to add to his DFC and bar. He, as much as anyone, had helped put paid to Rommel's plans in North Africa.

What has also to be remembered was that while we now know that almost every sailing of Axis shipping was noted through Ultra intercepts, to protect this secret information, the reconnaissance Spitfires had to be sent out to 'find' them, so that when later attacked, the Germans wouldn't begin to smell a rat. It wouldn't do to have the strike aircraft go out and 'get lucky' every time! If the Germans thought they had merely been unlucky enough to have their ships spotted, then the Ultra information remained safe.

When the 69 Squadron Spitfire pilots, like Les Colquhoun or Harry Coldbeck were sent out on some occasions, they were ordered to call in the sighting to Malta – in clear language – so that the Germans would intercept the message and know their ships had been spotted. While this was all part of the plot, it did, of course, put the recce pilots in extra danger by having their own position noted, but likewise, the Germans then knew for certain that a strike was not far off. Harry Coldbeck for one, having returned from his sortie would remember the looks on the faces of the Beaufort crews, when they were about to go on theirs. Sadly they knew the Germans had been alerted and were waiting for them. There could then be very little in the way of a surprise attack to help their chances of survival.

* * *

One Beaufort crew was to experience a unique adventure while flying from Malta. The skipper was a South African, Lieutenant Ted Strever SAAF, his navigator being Pilot Officer W M Dunsmore RAF, while the two Wireless Operator/Air Gunners were both New Zealanders – Sergeants J A Wilkinson and A R Brown.

The two NCO's had just recently been shot down with another crew, their pilot and navigator having been wounded. They now teamed up with Strever and Dunsmore and on 28 July 1942 were about to embark on Strever's third Beaufort sortie.

The target was the oil tanker *Monsivo*, heavily protected by Italian destroyers. Nine aircraft attacked and Strever appeared, like the others, to have missed his target, but the flak didn't miss him. The Beaufort was hit by a devastating hail of gunfire; Ted knowing at once that it was crippled. Before losing all control, he managed successfully to ditch the plane. All four men got out safely although it was touch-and-go whether Strever himself could get out but he just managed it and joined the others in the dinghy before the aircraft sank. Overhead a Malta Baltimore circled, probably sending out a position fix, but with Malta 300 miles away the chance of rescue was remote.

The hills of Greece were visible to the east and the crew began to paddle in that direction. Before long, however, a Cant Z506B floatplane landed nearby and took the men aboard. They were treated well and given cigarettes and brandy. The Cant flew to Preveza, about half way between the southern tip of Corfu and the northern one of Cephalonia. Here they were well fed and given the run of an officer's mess. When the evening meal came round, this also was a splendid spread, far superior to anything that Malta could possibly offer at that time. This was washed down with a plentiful supply of good wine. This was another luxury that Ted and his crew had long forgotten on Malta.

The Italian crew also found them good sleeping quarters. Apart from having guards posted at both ends of the corridor and also outside the windows, the treatment was more like honoured guests than prisoners of war. Also, of course, Ted and his crew had not been sure of even being picked up so it could be argued that the Cant crew had saved their lives.

Next morning, after the rare treat of a breakfast of eggs and real coffee, Ted Strever and his crew were put aboard another Cant 506B to begin their journey to Taranto. The Cant had a crew of four – two pilots, engineer and gunner/wireless operator. In addition there was an armed guard to keep an eye on the prisoners. This was a rather scruffy looking corporal carabiniere, armed with a revolver.

The Allied crew had come from far and wide to fight the war and they had no wish to spend the remainder of it in some prisoner of war camp. The corporal was probably unused to air travel for it was not long before he became air sick. This was the opportunity the prisoners had been hoping for. Sergeant Wilkinson led the attack and managed to wrestle the revolver away from the guard, handing it to Strever, who went forward to confront the pilot. The pilot – Lieutenant Gaetano Mastrodicaca of the 139a Maritime Recce Squadriglia – also had a gun and for a moment or two the pilots faced each other while the uncontrolled flying boat headed for the sea. In the end the Italian lieutenant gave way and Strever took over the plane.

There seemed to be no maps or charts on board and for a while the Beaufort crew let the second pilot fly while they tried to work out where they were, what fuel they had and what to do next. There was also a confrontation with the flight engineer who, at first, refused to turn on the aircraft's reserve fuel tanks, but with a threat by Strever to shoot the man, he gave way, although he said that by 1pm – 'Petroli fini!'

At first a course was set for Sicily in order to have some idea of where they were but when the toe of Italy appeared there seemed a good chance of reaching Malta. Strever took over the controls again, heading south west with fuel gauges showing almost zero. One o'clock passed without seeing the island but a new threat appeared – the threat of this Italian plane being picked up on radar and then intercepted by RAF fighters. Strever dived the flying boat low over the sea but in vain, for as Malta came into view, so too did a section of Spitfires from 603 Squadron.

These attacked, the Cant being hit in one wing – the 'successful' pilot being Sergeant Bill Young, a Rhodesian and a personal friend of Strever's! Never having had to land a flying boat on the water before, Strever had put the Italian skipper back into the pilot's seat and demanded he land immediately. It was only as the Italian had throttled back that the first Spitfire attacked, causing its fire to overshoot. Once on the water, Dunsmore had stripped off his white undervest and was waving it frantically as a gesture of surrender while Sergeant Brown visibly rotated the Cant's guns in order to show that they were not being fired.

The Cant landed about two miles off shore, between St Paul's Bay and Sliema. As it touched down the engines stopped – out of petrol! Before long an Air Sea Rescue boat – HSL 107 – came out to tow the plane to a mooring buoy.

The captured Cant held a couple of surprises when it was inspected. There was a suitcase full of money and a goodly supply of vino. However, that was somewhat reduced by the time that Strever and his crew had been taken ashore. It is thought that both RAF and Italian crews helped in this reduction.

All four men were decorated. Strever and Dunsmore being awarded DFCs, while DFMs went to Brown and Wilkinson. The pilot of the Baltimore, who had circled the dinghy, was flown by a personal friend of Sergeant Brown but he did not know it was his friend down in the sea until after he landed his aircraft back on Malta. He arranged for a cable to be sent to Brown's family back in New Zealand but, luckily, Brown was able to get back before it was sent. The Baltimore pilot was later Brown's best man at his wedding.

The subsequent great success by the Armies at Alamein owed much to the brave endeavours of the Beaufort squadrons, which, living under the appalling siege conditions of Malta, nevertheless attacked at every opportunity. The cost in lives was terrible especially among the low level aircrews but the job had to be done.

If the names of men such as Pat Gibbs and Arthur Aldridge are now the best remembered in Malta, there were dozens of others equally brave whose last glimpse of life was an enemy ship, a hail of flak and then the enveloping waters of the Mediterranean. Yet even the few who survived received little public recognition.

The seed that was planted in Malta by Pat Gibbs, especially his idea that deck clearing Beaufighters accompany the torpedo droppers, was to grow into the formidable Strike Wings of Coastal Command in England which, between 1943–45, were to cause havoc with enemy coastal shipping from Norway to the French coast. What had started as the sinking of Rommel's supplies to North Africa ended with the huge losses of ships along the enemy's North Sea coastal routes.

CHAPTER NINE

THE LADIES – GOD BLESS 'EM

It may come as a surprise to some that there were a number of women who served no less valiantly on Malta as did their male counterparts, although in very different ways.

Nellie Galea was half Maltese and half English, her father having been a distinguished Maltese Merchant Navy Captain, one who served well in WWI. Later he served in some senior post or harbour capacity in Malta. Her English mother died when Nellie was still quite young and she was brought up in England by an aunt, consequently she spoke perfect English and was virtually 100% English in thought.

Then, on 29 July, 1939, as a sixteen year old teenager, she made a visit to her father having bought a return ticket on the Commonwealth Line from Aberdeen. She still has the return half! With Germany and Britain at war by September, it was thought safer for her to remain on the island. Little did they know!

In Malta, Nellie learnt shorthand and typing, then began work for a glove manufacturer. She hated it, so when in August 1940 a call went out for clerks to assist the RAF, she was swift to apply, and, thanks to the good references from her employer, was equally swiftly taken on – and not just taken on. She found herself, still a young teenager, working for the Air Officer Admin (AOA), ie: for the No 2 in the RAF to the Air Officer Commanding (AOC). She was soon working for both.

Initially the RAF HQ was in South Street, Valletta. The arrival of Hugh Lloyd changed things. The workload increased and '...everyone now worked throughout the whole day – no more siesta time and soon all the offices were moved to the 'Ditch' where Hugh Pughe could keep an eye on us.'

Nellie worked tirelessly for three different AOA's and AOC's and didn't leave Malta until the end of April 1944. Her closeness to both positions meant that there were few, if any, secrets not known to her, and the author can personally attest that she proved to be a tower of strength and reliability. All her AOA's received the CBE and Nellie's BEM was richly deserved. Indeed, this could never have been written but for Nellie Galea because, due to her quick thinking, she unquestionably saved my life!

It was just after that wonderful ship the *Breconshire*[1] had made her last tragic journey. Nellie had a rare afternoon off and, hearing that a couple of officers from that ship were enquiring if a game of tennis was possible, Nellie, whom I had come to know because of my many orders which came direct from Hugh Pughe, I being 'in and out' of his office most days, asked if I could play. When I said yes, she borrowed clothes, rackets and balls, etc, from goodness-knows-where. She was a marvel at finding the most unobtainable items in Malta. I remember one time, when no soap was available, she managed to get me a cake of Bob Martins dark-green dog (antiflea) soap. (Most pets had by then ended up on someone's meal table!) It also served me as toothpaste!

So it was that, at the height of the March '42 blitz, three men and Nellie, all dressed in correct 'whites', started to play tennis on the nice court just behind the Sliema Club, looking to all the world like a pre-war social occasion.

Inevitably a raid soon started. Nellie and I by then, if not actually 'bomb happy' were at least bomb accustomed, having survived well over 1,000 raids. That afternoon's usual dive bombing affair was however, a relatively new experience for our two Naval types although, being men of the *Breconshire*, they had had their fair taste of bombardment at sea.

In those March days, if it wasn't your airfield being attacked and if you could see from the dive bombers that someone else was 'getting it', there was almost a savage satisfaction in watching Ju 87s and 88s peeling off to give someone else a pasting. ('Poor old Ta Kali again' – or some such remark) But suddenly Nellie cried out, 'Look Tony, how about this one?'

I followed her pointing finger and saw to my absolute horror, a Ju 88 diving deliberately at the Sliema Club. It was almost a legitimate target as the chances were that some officers would be there; it was strictly an 'officers only' club. So obvious was it that I was about to be blasted to bits, that mind and muscles froze. Clearly this was 'Goodbye earth!' But Nellie's mind was razor sharp. She grabbed me and propelled me away from the court at

---

[1] *Breconshire* had made several solo runs to Malta and did as much as any other ship to keep Malta alive with oil and supplies.

speed, hustling us both under an outside stone stairway that led to the flat roof of the Clubhouse.

A single bomb – later estimated at about 1,500 kg – all that the Junkers could carry, hit slap on the tennis court. We must have been no more than 30 yards away. Part of the Club came down about our ears, the noise shattering all immediate thought and left us stunned. The cloud of dust which totally enveloped us was so thick that, although we had instinctively clung together (life's last embrace?), it was quite impossible even to see one another, let alone anything else.

As we were the only occupants of the Club, and once we had regained our senses, we scrambled clear, careful not to disturb more dust, rubble and large lumps of blasted Maltese limestone blocks. Incredibly, although the tennis court was now just one vast crater, the two balls we had dropped as we dashed for cover, were right on the edge of the hole, exactly where we'd dropped them when the Ju 88 released its bomb!

We retrieved what we could of our normal clothing from the remains of the changing rooms, then made our way to the ferry steps to find a dghaissa man to row us back to Valletta. We had scarcely gone half way down to the water's edge when the next raid began. We went down into a shelter but very quickly, by mutual consent emerged again, hating the all pervading smell of fear, mixed with sweaty bodies and urine. It was an experience I never wanted to repeat.

Nellie Galea was a lot more than just a faithful confidential secretary to the two air chiefs on Malta; there was little she did not know about RAF operations and the men who were carrying them out. On one occasion she helped to save an aeroplane, short of fuel. It had engine trouble and ice problems as it tried to get back to Malta. The crew had very little idea where they were and after over ten hours were rapidly running out of fuel. They were sending out SOS calls but receiving no help.

The ASV and other aerials had iced up, but by using her initiative (it was dawn, when few Ops room people had surfaced), Nellie rang up a man she knew who was in charge of a radar station near Kalafrana. Flying Officer Bob Povey swung his aerials in an unusual direction and picked up an unidentified blip to the south east. Nellie went to the Ops Room with the range and bearing that Bob had given and persuaded them to pass this to the lost Wellington crew.

The Wimpey crew, having no other option, altered course as

shown by the 'fix' and with fuel gauges showing zero, one engine faltering, managed to scrape into Luqa after more than 11 hours; a record for a Wimpey? It is not often that a pilot's life is saved twice by a quick thinking teenage girl in the midst of a hot war. Once on a tennis court and again in a Wellington!

Thank you Nellie Galea BEM. That time you saved my crew as well as me.

* * *

Mary Bates was a nurse at Imtarfa Military Hospital, a building which overlooked the airfield of Ta Kali. She kept a diary which I have been able to read and receive permission to quote from. Even the brief extracts here show a vivid picture of daily life on Malta in 1942:

> Saturday March 21st, 1942. A real Ta Kali blitz at about 10 am, when three bombs fell on Imtarfa. One killed seven Durham Light Infantry men and injured seven others. They were asleep after guarding German prisoners at night. A second bomb demolished the Imtarfa Club and the third fell near the reception block close to a slit trench. Two patients in G Block were injured and an ambulance destroyed. My men were bricks in E Block! I found Private Boothe lying down beside me in the wet of the recently washed floor of the verandah! We didn't notice the blast so very much although two of my wards had doors blown off and locked cupboards were wrenched open.
>
> In the afternoon I had gone to tea when another attack began. It became alarming and I went down to the deep rock shelter for the first time. This time, there were no casualties. In the same raid bombs dropped at Rabat and at the Point de Vue Hotel. Seven officers were killed. Amongst those were Waterfield, who came out with us in the *Reine Del Paciico*, and Junior, the 19 year old American pilot whom everybody liked so much.[2]
>
> Sunday, March 23rd. Ships in! (*Talabot* and *Pampas*). The *Clan Campbell* was sunk on the way and the *Breconshire* bombed through the engine room just off Malta and was

[2] Pilot Officer Eddie 'Junior' Streets, 126 Squadron, lost a leg and was blinded, later dying from his injuries.

unable to be brought into harbour as all her electricity and steering gear was out of order. The *Pampas*, and the Norwegian ship *Talabot* made the grade however. Air raids for the next three days were therefore centred on the harbour. The destroyer *Woolsac* struck a mine and broke in half.

March 25th. A quieter night. Two Sisters left in a Wellington bomber at midnight – their sixth attempt at going.

March 26th. Raids on Valletta and Floriana this morning. The Norwegian merchantman was set on fire, the *Plum-Leaf* (tanker and empty) was sunk and the *Pampas* was hit. I cycled down to the Melita Hotel and met John Pearce RNVR. He had to be back on board his minesweeper by 6.00 pm so we decided to go to Hajiar Kim. We only had time to rush round it like a couple of American tourists and eat our tea before getting back. As we crossed Luqa aerodrome there was a tremendous barrage over the harbour but by the time we reached Marsa Creek where we parted, it was over. The poor ship was absolutely blazing by that time.

March 27th. The *Breconshire* had to be scuttled but the *Pampas* was being unloaded rapidly. The burning Norwegian ship with explosive cargo had her side blown out by a brave engineer Petty Officer to let in the water in order to prevent a terrible explosion, which would have shaken Valletta to her very foundations. The cargo, much of it, will also thus be saved. Rome Radio afterwards gave out that the Germans had lost 45 planes on this particular day, so what must they have lost on certain other occasions lately?

March 31st. Meat difficult to obtain. Bully beef substituted. No jam. Salmon one tin to four people. Bread rationed.

April 2nd. The 'Times of Malta' says that we damaged or destroyed 27 German planes yesterday. The ack-ack got five for certain. A very nasty raid on Luqa at 5.00 pm. The chief concern at the moment is a slight outbreak of diphtheria. Two soldiers working in the laboratory have it and three surgical cases from the 45th have been transferred.

April 4th. We can pretty well depend upon a raid about every three hours these days. A bad blitz on the harbour at mid-day when the Kingston and a submarine were hit and we had many casualties from a tunnel which caught the blast from a couple of bombs very badly. 60 bombs fell in the actual dockyard. We took about 40 of the casualties, 10 died – all blast cases.

April 5th. The minesweeper Abingdon – John's ship – was beached after being hit.

April 6th. Every ship in the harbour has now been hit with the exception of *HMS Penelope* which has had many near misses. The heaviest raid was at 6.00 pm when five waves of 12 attacked the harbour and Hal Far. Six casualties only admitted to us and none of them theatre cases.

April 8th. I went up to the main theatre to watch a list in the evening. Four cases had been done when I left at 11.15 pm. A pilot with lacerations of legs and scalp; a RE sergeant with burns of face, arms and back; a sailor with lacerations of buttock and other minor lacerations; a maritime gunner with compound fracture of tibia and fibula, amputated above the knee. That was Byatt off the cruiser *Kingston*. He and his colleague both with Oerliken guns have hit a large number of planes lately – he claims 20 himself!

HMS Penelope made a get away at 9.00 pm. Captain Nicholl took a volunteer crew of 100 only as she was not exactly sea worthy. The after steering gear was being used and water was having to be pumped out all the time. The men, wearing bathing trunks, were said to be up to their waists in water. 150 out of 200 who were to have been left behind, scrambled aboard at the last minute! The following afternoon there was a signal to say that she was being continually attacked from the air somewhere off Sardinia and that she was running short of ammunition. Actually her gun barrels were worn out and were due to be renewed when she left Malta. Later we rejoiced to hear that she had arrived at Gibraltar having been met by the Navy. Ship now known as *HMS Pepperpot*.

Tuesday, April 14th. One long alert all day, 5.30 am – 8.30 pm! Such a racket at 1.15 pm when Spitfires and Me 109s appeared to be chasing each other up and down between the barrack blocks! Hurricanes, Beaufighters and Beaufort bombers are reputed to have been trying to get in all day. One of our pilots, after baling out, came down on the rocks below the cliffs at Dingli. Flying Officer Jones let down a rope over the cliff's edge and fetched him up.

April 17th. George Cross for the Island fortress of Malta.

April 19th. After lunch I decided to cycle down to Lapsi with Mary Perkins. It was lovely in the sun on the rocks. There was the usual tea time raid so we ate our tea inside the barn as there was some machine gunning and enemy fighters were flying out, quite low, from the side. A ship was burning in the harbour and we were told that there were still no serviceable Spitfires when to our joy we suddenly saw at least nine circling round. They had just come in! Eggs 3/6d a dozen (during the food shortage they went up to 2/6d each, at one time). Meat very difficult to obtain.

April 20th. Such excitement! A formation of 12 Spitfires roared over the hospital after the morning raid and many others are here we understand. There was a battle-royal at 1.00 –2.00 pm, when the barrage was heavier than any we had ever known over the hospital. The gunners were delighted yesterday when their communications were down and they were firing with local control only. 17 planes were claimed down or damaged. Our moment today came when 190 aircraft were said to have crossed the coast. Fighters harassed the bombers and they dropped bombs all over the place. Our officer's mess got a direct hit. A 1,000lb bomb bounced near the main hospital and fell up against the mortuary, but did not go off. Two other smaller ones fell about 20 or 30 feet away from it and did not go off either. Lieutenant Ellis GC, having been in hospital a fortnight with blast injuries and fractured base of the skull, volunteered to deal with the large bomb and went down in his dressing gown and took the fuse out. All patients were put down the big shelter for the night. Poor dears – many of them with dreadful wounds.

Saturday, April 25th. The first raid, 7.00 – 7.30 am, caught many people going to work. It was directed against camps, gun positions, etc, and the 45th got hit and the 39th General Hospital was demolished except for four hutments. Four patients and an orderly were killed. A good many casualties were brought in.

April 30th. Me 109s and Spitfires rushed up and down over the barrack hospital in the morning raid and a hand grenade was thrown between E and G Blocks which gave the spectators a nasty fright! Every time one of our fighters tried to land at Ta Kali a Me 109 swooped down on it with cannon fire.[3]

Sunday, May 3rd. Had a German prisoner admitted to G upper Block (he hated the raids!). You cannot stop our men from treating people as they find them! They loved Weber[4] and his bed was usually surrounded!

May 4th. Bread ration $10^{1}/_{2}$ ozs per person per day (later it was reduced to 7 ozs, at that time we could not get many vegetables and no potatoes. Then we were rather hungry).

May 6th. Some patients were evacuated by air. They got away in spite of many raids all night.

May 7th. Lord Gort arrived from Gibraltar to take over the Governorship of the island.

May 8th. Found six new battle casualties in the ward, but not such bad ones.

Mary's diary draws quite a picture, doesn't it?

* * *

The Honourable Mabel Strickland OBE, was a truly remarkable character and did much to raise the morale of both the British and Maltese peoples on the battered island. 'Miss Mabel' – the name by which she was widely known, was the founder, proprietor and editor of the daily English language newspaper, the famous 'Times of Malta'. She also edited and produced a Maltese paper called 'It Berqua'. On Sundays she issued the 'Sunday Times.'

---

[3] Author's note. So ended April 1942, Malta's worst month of the war. 6,729 tons of bombs had been dropped and nearly all on either the harbours around Valletta or the three airfields of Luqa, Hal Far and Ta Kali. Among the 550 killed were 208 servicemen. The enemy's average daily sortie rate was approx 380, ie: 11,474 in all during the 30 days. On some days the alert was in force for 18 hours. The weight of bombs dropped was greater than that dropped in any one month during the Battle of Britain - for the entire UK!

[4] This was probably Gefr. Fritz Weber, rear gunner of a Ju 87 from III/StG3 shot down on the 3rd by a Spitfire of 603 Squadron. The Stuka crashed near Zonqur, the pilot being killed.

Miss Mabel was the daughter of Lord Strickland GCMG, who, as well as having been Prime Minister of Malta between 1927–32, was also a wealthy landholder in Malta, via a family inheritance. As a result, Miss Mabel was born in Malta, probably in the Parisio Palace at Lija, where the Stricklands lived.

However, she was educated and brought up in Australia where her father was Governor of New South Wales at various times, as well as other States, including Tasmania. Mabel Strickland served briefly as a cypher officer in the First World War. Although there were other children in the family, including older daughters, it was Mabel – the third daughter – who seems to have become almost the ruling force in the family. It was she who persuaded her father, after his last Governorship, to settle in Malta for by then she had become passionately attached to the islands and had already made it her lifelong crusade to try to ensure that the links between Malta and Britain should be retained and strengthened. At one time she was even advocating, vociferously, that Malta become a part of the UK.

Throughout the whole siege, the 'Times of Malta' and 'Sunday Times' kept the troops in the island well informed about events in the war both locally and elsewhere. Her papers appeared with unfailing regularity and were always factual and fair. Her influence spread beyond mere publishing and she was also likely to voice her opinions to people such as Winston Churchill or Lord Louis Mountbatten. In such a small island it was well nigh impossible to ignore a person of her drive.

Physically, Mabel Strickland – in her 50's during the siege – was a large woman with ample breasts. She was fond of lifting up these expansive protuberances and exclaiming: 'But for these, I would be Prime Minister!' It is perhaps no great surprise she never married. One 'man' in any such alliance would have been more than enough!

Apart from her newspapers, she also found time to entertain the men serving on the island. It was a considerable honour to be invited to her tennis parties. She proved an excellent hostess while also advancing her ideas about how the Maltese and British peoples should continue to work hand-in-hand after the war had been won.

Flight Lieutenant Syd Collins, who served at different times as Station Adjutant at Luqa, then Ta Kali, had clear recollections of this formidable and fiercely patriotic lady. He was also a frequent guest at those tennis parties. He had become one of her favourites because he had answered her call for a means of recharging the batteries of the hearing aid which her stepmother – the second Lady Strickland – needed in order to hear anything.

As Syd has written: 'Because it was for Miss Mabel, it was impossible to say 'No'. However, replacement batteries were unobtainable but the 'Adj' – as she always called him, managed to get the existing ones recharged thanks to the ingenuity of the Ta Kali Station Electrical Engineering Officer. Moreover, because it was her, Collins was periodically able to borrow the Station Commander's car to collect and return them!

In return, Miss Mabel, was persuaded by the Adj to extend her invitations to 'other ranks'. These parties were almost a throw back to pre-war days with Miss Mabel pouring out the tea from an exquisite solid silver teapot with delicate china tableware on display. This was at a time when, due to normal supplies having been broken, both officers and men were using sawn-off beer bottles for normal drinking glasses! In the end, Syd managed to obtain permission for her tennis courts to be used exclusively by junior officers, NCOs and other ranks every Thursday afternoon. All this, plus the use of her showers, was a great morale booster. For a few brief hours we were transported into a saner world.

Mabel lived on until aged nearly 90 and although the war is to some a fading memory, there can be few, if any, servicemen who served or even visited Malta, who doesn't remember with gratitude the daily appearance of her newspapers, knowing that raids had not stopped production. One cannot help but wonder what she might have achieved if she had been born a man. Without her massive breasts, almost anything might have been possible.

* * *

Christina Ratcliffe had a very different upbringing from that of the Hon. Mabel Strickland, but in determination and energy they had much in common.

Mary Christine Ratcliffe (she was known as Mary at home) was born in the north of England where her father was the owner, or manager, of a smallish cotton mill at Duckinfield, Hyde, near Manchester. She had two bothers. Secretive about her birth date, it seems likely she was born around 1910–11 but most people thought she was younger than the 'near thirty' she was in June 1940. Unquestionably she looked younger!

It seems that from an early age she was aware that she belonged to a wider world than that which surrounded her environment, and with boundless energy and high spirits, she was determined to explore the wider world beyond her father's mill. At school she was well above the average in intelligence and became a prefect. Thanks to her father's position, and unlike so many in the depression years, she had no difficulty in securing a job – in her father's mill. But the big world outside beckoned.

Her chance came when she won a crossword competition, the prize money taking her to London where she enrolled herself in a dancing academy. She studied hard but was soon to discover that she lacked the essential talent to become a first class dancer. Despite her sparkling good looks, the required health and energy, her teachers advised her to give it up. 'You will never go far!' they warned. It was a verdict that she was determined to prove wrong. What the teachers seemed to have overlooked was that very determined chin which appears in all her photographs.

Now calling herself Christine, she began to 'go places' by accepting dancing engagements that others would not accept. With her own self confidence she was soon dancing in various clubs, not only in England but in Germany, France (Paris), Italy and Spain. She was able to pick up the local language and her brain did the rest; prospering by going where others dared not go.

Her first brush with war came during the Spanish Civil War while dancing in Barcelona. After many adventures which she undoubtedly enjoyed, she was evacuated, along with other British nationals, in a Royal Navy destroyer. Something else happened in Spain; she was now Christina, changing the 'e' for an 'a'. It was a name which she used ever afterwards to such an extent that not many who knew her in later life, realised that she was 100% British, although she always spoke in an excellent English accent.

The Mediterranean fascinated her and, with considerable bravado, she accepted engagements in Morocco, Tunisia and other places where many others would not even think of venturing. An incident in Tunisia gives some idea of her forcefulness. When a cafe owner failed to pay her the contractual salary, she took him to court, pleading her case in French, not only winning but ending up engaged to the youthful French Judge! It was soon after this that Christina accepted a dubious engagement in Malta, dancing in a downtown cafe (most probably in the Gut), which concentrated in giving British sailors a 'good time' while in port! The engagement was short, due to end on or about June 20th, 1940, when she planned to return to Tunis and her fiancé. Mussolini's declaration of war on June 10th, changed many things but few had their lives so altered as did Christina Ratcliffe.

Abruptly, the clubs and cabarets were closed. Valletta's streets were blacked out – the lights of Malta going out for the next three years, while Christina, and other entertainers, were out of a job. Worse still, it was soon evident that, until the war was over, there was no means whereby an unimportant civilian could leave the island. With no money and no job, Christina, along with a couple of British artists, Cecil and Babs Roche, with whom she shared a flat in Floriana, set up a makeshift concert party which they called the Whizz Bangs. They toured round the island to the various military bases and were an instant success, although their only income was obtained by passing a hat round at the end of the shows. However, their success helped the troupe increase in number and they were soon adopted by the NAAFI which brought them a regular salary.

Christina next answered the call for English speaking volunteers to help man the telephones in the underground RAF/RN War Operations Room.

Here her quick intelligence and lively personality were soon noticed and though still dancing almost daily with the Whizz Bangs, she became a plotter in the RAF nerve centre. Here she helped display the positions of enemy aircraft as they were picked up by radar, thus assisting the Fighter Controller to position his fighters to intercept incoming raids. Promotion to Captain of 'D' Watch followed and not until further promoted to Assistant to the Controller, was Christina obliged to give up her role in the Whizz Bangs.

Long before this, however, she had become the close and devoted companion of the remarkable Adrian Warburton. As his decorations increased it was Christina who would sew the ribbons and rosettes on to his battledress uniforms. Warby had first met Christina at a party after a friend of her's, a brave French airman, Jacques Douvelles, had been shot down when flying in an aircraft of the Squadron to which Warby also belonged. Jacques had come from Tunis so he and

Christina, with whom he could speak French, had a common interest.

For Christina, her meeting Warby was a case of love at first sight. Warby had recently been restored to piloting duties and was beginning to make a name for himself. Warby said how sorry he was that her French friend was missing. She found herself gazing into his incredible blue eyes and at once abandoned any plans she may have had of getting back to her fiancé in Tunis. Soon the pair were sharing a flat in Floriana and it was here that Warby was able to relax, forget the war for a short while and generally recharge his batteries. As George Burges has said: 'I'm sure that Christina was an enormous help to Warby. She helped to bring him out of his shell.'

Certainly for her, there would never be another man to equal him – a fact she confided to the author. Certainly she never married. In his case, Warby was already married; although unhappily. After Warby's death, she had many opportunities to marry, but never did. Another young plotter was Marion Gould, who said, 'We all took an interest in Warby and Christina, they were such a glamorous couple.'

The pair of them were also used for publicity purposes when visiting VIPs needed to be shown around. This is, perhaps, why the Imperial War Museum today has over 50 photographs of her going about her daily business: bargaining for scarce rations; carrying pails of water; dancing in her Spanish costume; dancing in the chorus; alongside her Warby while showing visitors around; as a plotter and even sitting up in bed reading the morning edition of 'Miss Mabel's' newspaper.

It was no surprise when Christina received the British Empire Medal in recognition of her official and unofficial work. Her official work in Fighter Control alone justified the award but her value to the morale of the island was every bit as high, especially to a very special pilot.

It seems doubtful if Christina ever fully got over the loss of Warby in April 1944 and accepted she would never see him again. By then she was known to his family and she treasured the cable of congratulations from his mother on the award of her BEM. Yet her post-war life was far from mundane. For many years she was the civilian secretary to successive RAF Station Commanders at Luqa. In addition, with her usual abundant energy, she also owned and ran a cafe in Valletta – Cafe Christina. However, as the years passed by, she became more and more a recluse and avoided various attempts of journalists and authors to seek her out. I was singularly fortunate, having also served on Malta and had known her Warby. She was writing her own life story, but unfortunately it was never finished and is now, since her death in 1988, probably lost for ever. It was entitled 'Carve Malta on my Heart.' She wrote superbly well; I know, for I was privileged to be allowed to read it. She remained in Malta.

Her last few years were not happy ones, trying to drown her loneliness in alcohol, she became withdrawn and impoverished. She died alone in her flat and was not discovered until several weeks had passed. Having lost touch with her family, she was buried in a communal grave[5]. Later, the Sunday Times of Malta printed my long tribute to her. It included the epithet: 'She had much to give and she gave her all.'

---

[5] The author has since discovered relatives who are taking appropriate steps regarding reburial, etc.

Luqa – May 1943. A brand new Spitfire IX *Eric Hughes*

Adrian Warbuton, in American Air Corps uniform, is shown the instruments of a USAAC P-38 PR Lightning, which he is about to unofficially operate. Lt Joe Scalpone USAF is the instructor. *Imperial War Museum*

Warburton in typical casual dress, shows Lt Col Solodovnik around Malta. The colonel was the first Russian officer to visit Malta during the blitz. *Imperial War Museum*

Tropicalised Spitfire V, flown by Squadron Leader Grant, taking off from the carrier *Eagle*, for Malta. *NWMA*

HMS Aurora, the leading ship of the successful Force K. Her commander was Captain W G Agnew RN. *Aurora* and *Penelope* were light cruisers, 5,270 tons. *Imperial War Museum*

No one deserves higher praise (and a well-earned personal George Cross) than the RAF Officer Flt Lt Dickinson who dealt with hundreds of unexploded bombs. *Imperial War Museum*

in obsolescent Hurricane I's without any radar assistance at all.

The Beaus were not just equipped with AI but also carried a formidable punch, with four 20 mm cannons and six .303 machine guns. Provided the pilot was on target it was almost certain that when a Beau opened fire, that was the end of the raider. Being able to stalk without the aid of searchlights, meant that the crews of the Ju 88s or SM79s would have no warning whatsoever. Their first intimation that they had been detected would be a blistering burst of fire from behind. Swiftly the hostile aircraft would fall in flames. Many a Malta citizen or Malta veteran can recall with savage satisfaction seeing the sight of a 'flamer' falling from the dark sky. Having put up with so many raids, it was a great boost to morale.

With a crew of two, the Beau was deadly. The AI operator had to be every bit as skilful as his pilot and more often than not, the success or failure of every mission lay in his hands. He would be the one directing the pilot to the correct position for a stern attack.

Other 89 Squadron crews eventually took the place of the original trio but not before these three crews had accounted for 19 enemy aircraft destroyed with others damaged. As was so often the case in Malta, the Beau's crews were a happy mixture of Commonwealth volunteers. The all-Canadian crew of Flying Officer R C 'Moose' Fumerton DFC and Sergeant L P S Bing (later commissioned) established a good reputation with seven victories in June/July 1942. Another crew consisted of the Australian Pilot Officer M C Shipard and Sergeant Doug Oxby (he later becoming a top scoring AI operator as a flight lieutenant with the DSO DFC DFM and bar). They gained three kills over Malta that July. Flight Lieutenant H G Edwards with Sergeant J R Phillipson, were to gain five kills, while Pilot Officer N E Reeves and Sergeant A A O'Leary claimed another five.

The honeymoon of easy kills didn't last overlong. The enemy soon got wind of the Beau's radar and began to jam the frequency. This led to more advanced AI sets being used, inevitably followed by more advanced jamming. But in this electronic war, the Germans were always one step behind.

Beaufighters of a different kind would occasionally be sent from Egypt, and once from the UK, when especially required during critical periods but only when the island could provide the petrol necessary for this quite thirsty fighter/fighter-bomber. Essentially these Beaus were long range fighters but, as was Malta's custom, most fighters came to be used for bombing with locally made racks fitted. These were all daylight fighters and they tended to arrive whenever a relieving convoy was due to approach. Such aircraft were able to protect the convoy at distances beyond those attainable by the Hurricanes and Spitfires. Those last few days were always critical for the convoys.

The big naval ships would have turned back for Gibraltar or Alexandria by this time. The remnants of the merchant ships, now only protected by destroyers and perhaps light cruisers, would be struggling to get past the 'bomb alleys' which existed in the Straits between Cap Bon and Pantellaria, or between Crete and the North African coast. The long-range Beaus could protect the ships for a whole day before the Spits and Hurris could take over such duties.

These heavily armed Beaufighters were also put to good use, thanks to the insistence of Patrick Gibbs, the dynamic leader of the Beauforts. He used them as low level attack planes against the enemy's escorting destroyers of their convoys to Tripoli and Benghazi – Tobruk too when it fell to the Axis forces. Pat Gibbs argued with logic, that the horrific losses which his Beauforts were suffering would be reduced if a number of Beaufighters flew alongside the slower torpedo carrying Beauforts and, seconds before the attack began, the Beaus would, literally, clear the decks of the Italian destroyers and the armed merchantmen, by blasting them with their withering weight of fire. These helpful Beaus came from a 252 Squadron detachment, which was based on Luqa as early as June 1941, but quickly moved on to Egypt after some early attacks on Sicily and Greece.

No 252 Squadron also had a detachment on Malta in February 1942 for convoy patrol duties. Detachments from 272 Squadron also appeared at Luqa at odd times during early 1942; not only defending convoys but attacking airfields on Sicily. In late 1942, 272 were at Ta Kali under its dynamic leader Wing Commander J K Buchanan DSO DFC & bar, and were able to get in amongst the German and Italian transport aircraft desperately trying to get supplies to Tunisia.

A detachment of 235 Squadron was made into 227 Squadron at Luqa in August 1942, which then operated from Ta Kali in November. It flew strike missions against Axis convoys as well as escort sorties to Beauforts. Like 272 Squadron, 227 were also successful against the later transport flights made by the German and Italian air forces, Buck Buchanan being its CO too, for a period in late 1943.

In the end, the deck-clearing Beaus came to be attached to Pat Gibbs' Beaufort unit, comprised from 39, 86 and 217 Beaufort Squadrons' survivors. This further strengthened the degree of close co-operation required. Again at Pat Gibbs' insistence, some of these low level Beaus were fitted with locally made bomb racks so that they could additionally carry a small number of 250 or 500 lb bombs. These added to the carnage that the Beauforts were able to create. The bomb attacks were also made at mast height, requiring an 11-second delay fuse, so that the Beaus would not blow themselves up as they went over the target ship.

One technique used by the Beaus as low level bombers was 'skip-bombing'. Over the flat calm of the Mediterranean, a bomb dropped at low level would skip along the surface: a deadly version of Ducks and Drakes. Thus, if dropped close to the ship, there was every chance that it would eventually strike the superstructure of the ship. The only snag was that the bomb, being more streamlined that the aircraft, would tend to 'fly' along with the aircraft, even to overtake it! As a result, the pilot, after dropping, would find himself in extremely close formation with the deadly weapon. This led to some frantic avoiding actions! Another snag was that the flat calm of the sea, with no definition for the eyes, led to a number of Beaus striking the sea with their aircraft's propellers – usually, however, getting away with it.

The author used the same low level skip bombing technique at night when, on rare occasions, I was given bombs as well as flares and maximum fuel. However, nobody told me about the habit of the bombs to fly in immediate formation with my Wellington. As it was night time I did not notice their flight path. A case of ignorance being bliss! My bombs too had 11-second delay fuses – fortunately![2] The respective AOCs on Malta were always reluctant to allow any useful aeroplane to lie idle on Malta, as the reader will by now have become aware. Beaufighters sent there just for one special task tended to remain awhile. Some, it is reported, were used for intruder raids upon enemy airfields, both by day and by night. Others had 'field days' when later they were sent out to intercept large

---

[2] Or else I would have blown my Wellington and self to pieces when hitting the *Amersterdam*, 8,970 tons, on the night of 9 November 1941.

formations of Ju 52s, SM 82s or even the giant Me 323s ferrying men and fuel to North Africa. Post-war research has shown that at least 800 enemy troops were lost during their transportation to, or from, Tunisia, along with tons of high priority supplies. In all the Germans lost, from all causes, the best part of 300 Ju 52s during various phases of the Tunisian campaign.

One Beaufighter (daylight) pilot, was Cas de Bounevialle, who became a member of 227 Squadron. His first recollection of Malta, a not uncommon one, was the hearty welcoming which he received from the bed bugs in the Poorhouse where he was billeted:- 'They considered newcomers like me as a very welcome addition to their rations,' he recalls.

Cas's account of an adventure of the Canadian pilot, Flight Lieutenant Dallas Schmidt – known as 'Smithy' to everyone – and his navigator, Andy Campbell, a Scot, makes interesting reading. Smithy, who in Cas's eyes was the outstanding pilot of 227 Squadron, and Cas, went out in search of and to attack enemy coastal shipping. The date, which they will not forget, was Christmas Day, 1942.

> We found a pair of heavily armed F-boats (300 tons or so), big barges and a smaller schooner. We attacked. I hit mine all over but didn't see what happened to it. Smithy's was sinking when we left. His aircraft had been hit and he had lost all elevator and rudder control. He managed to stay airborne by use of throttles and by moving Andy back and forth.
>
> The Beau indulged itself in assorted aerobatics but kept on gaining height. About 50 miles from Malta, Smithy thought he had lost all control and told Andy to bale out. Andy did so but forgot to take his K-type dinghy. He told me later that once in the water, as he had nothing else to do, he decided to swim to the island! Fortunately for him, Smithy had alerted Malta of the situation and the rescue launch was already on its way. Thanks to carrying a two-star red cartridge with him, Andy was found and picked up.

Meanwhile, the Beau had come to its senses and Smithy arrived over Malta at 17,000 feet. Once over the island, he too 'hit the silk' but was nearly written off by the Beau continuing its crazy evolutions all around him until eventually it crashed.

Dallas Schmidt was also successful in shooting down an Italian

Cant Z1007 bis, on his very first Malta sortie – 28 August, 1942. On 17 September he put a 500 lb bomb amidships, into the 1,237 ton tanker *Carbonia*, which later sank. And long before he helped in the rescue of his own navigator as mentioned above, he saved the life of another squadron navigator. A Beau had gone into the sea, taking the pilot down with it, but the rear-man had struggled free. Schmidt saw the man was in trouble and dropped him a dinghy tied to his own Mae West, and later he was rescued, although the man had to stay in the dinghy overnight. The next day it was Smithy who relocated the dinghy, circling until a launch arrived.

Some idea of the casualties suffered by the Beaus comes from Cas:

> We went back into Malta on 6th November, 1942 with 17 crews – 34 men. When we came out in February 1943, there were less than a dozen of us left. Two crews had become tour expired, while the rest, including a number of replacement crews, were either dead or, in a very few cases, were prisoners of war.

As night fighters, the Beaufighters operating out of Malta, are credited with 60 night bombers destroyed and these losses did much to curtail the number of night raids. Their successes were a morale booster to the island.

Without doubt having Beaus attack alongside Beauforts, enabled many a torpedo pilot to drop his 'fish' more accurately and, equally important, saved many lives among the torpedo airmen. The help the Beaus were also able to give incoming ship convoys was also invaluable. Who knows? Without the extra protection that these long-range fighters were able to provide, maybe none of the ships of Operation Pedestal and Operation Harpoon might have reached Malta.

Beaufighter attacks against enemy airfields did much to unnerve the enemy and, of course, the famous PR Beau – T4705 – in Warburton's hands, enabled Hugh Pughe Lloyd to read the enemy's every intention at a time when no other photo-recce source was so readily available.

One day, it is told, the charismatic Warburton arrived at his Beau to discover an unexploded bomb alongside. He promptly borrowed a spanner from an airman and set about removing the bomb's fuse. 'Mind what you do with that spanner,' called out the airman, 'it's on my charge!'

CHAPTER ELEVEN

GROUNDCREW III

Four airmen have contributed to this chapter: Harry Duerden, who had been with the Fleet Air Arm early in the war; Owen Howell, from Wales; Philip Lewis, an RAF defence expert officer and James Ward.

Airman Harry Deurden learnt much about himself – and life in general – during an early wartime spell servicing Swordfish aircraft of 815 FAA Squadron, aboard the carrier *HMS Illustrious*. One of the first things he discovered, aged only 19, was he didn't qualify for the traditional daily tot of rum served to most of the men. When later he did qualify, he didn't want it but he was willing to accept the alternative of threepence per day in lieu. That horrified the 'old salts' of the navy, and one promptly offered him a shilling a day for his tot!

Harry rejoined the RAF in January 1941, full of praise for the lessons he had picked up from the Navy boys, but glad he had missed the subsequent bombing of the *Illustrious* in the Mediterranean, which killed over 100 of his former companions. After a spell in a transit camp, where he spent his 21st birthday, he found himself appointed to a 'special assignment' of trained electricians. Although kitted out with clothes more suitable for the arctic or for Russia, the unit's surprise can be imagined when they were finally told they were going to Malta!

Once on the island their task was to set up a new VHF and other W/T radio stations. They arrived in September 1941, during a lull in the bombing, so life began pleasantly enough. Warm sunshine, a chance to swim while air raids were only mildly troublesome. In fact the only tragedy was when a friend was drowned whilst swimming.

Then, after a pleasant six weeks at Kalafrana, Harry was posted to Command HQ, Valletta, where he lived in a Salvation Army hostel, and was able to 'enjoy' the dubious pleasures of the Gut. Early in the new year of 1942 Harry, the ADC's batman and another pal, rented a flat in Floriana, by pooling their Living Out allowances. Having missed being a casualty on the *Illustrious* he now just missed a second chance of serious injury or death as, just after he left the flat one Sunday morning, it was bombed. The flat was destroyed and one of his pals killed while still in bed.

He was later to experience and see the devastation of Luqa and the Safi Strip. Describing the damage, a colleague who had been there throughout and had seen the cookhouse demolished again and again, remarked that: 'If two consecutive meals were served in the same dining room, then Luqa was enjoying a good day!'

When promoted to corporal, Harry Duerden and some friends decided to 'do the Gut', starting with the 'British Queen' at the top and then work their way down every bar, drinking whatever they could get hold of. Worse for wear they found themselves at a shilling a night lodging house, waking with such a thirst that they all knelt by the bath, which due to water shortage, was kept filled for every household need, drinking down the water like horses at a trough!

Harry experienced the sheer horror of a bombing attack out in the open at Safi Strip, too far away from a shelter to get to in time, and the experience of hard-tack biscuits. With the latter, one had to leave them soaking in water, then with a little black chocolate added, the mixture was baked in a tin and usually eaten before going to bed in order to quell the hunger pains which often prevented sleep.

He also experienced 'butterfly' anti-personnel bombs, delayed action bombs and an absolutely frightening rocket bomb attack which descended with a terrifying scream to scare the daylights out of even the most hardy men.[1] When rumours of invasion came and everyone was issued with rifles, morale was at a new low.

During the bad winter of 1941–42, there was scarcely an established building still standing. Some men lived in makeshift quarters of newly quarried stone while others had to endure the cold and wet weather in unheated tents.

Things finally began to look up in the early spring and with the arrival of the Spitfires, everyone had new heart. With the arrival of 60 of Britain's finest fighters on 9 May, Harry recalls:

> The next few hours produced some of the finest exhibitions of aerial combat seen in any war. I cannot recall the numbers of enemy aircraft destroyed in the next two days but I do recall the sense of total relief to know that we had an equitable force and that our humiliation was over. We were back in business.
>
> I had a bird's eye view of the developing supremacy of the RAF, having climbed, along with others, the 100 foot

[1] The author's memory of these screaming rocket bombs is still vivid. As he typed these words 50 years later, the hairs behind his neck seemed to bristle.

aerial masts to get a better view. The newly established domination of the skies by the RAF brought a kind of warm security and calm over the whole island.

The feeling that the worst was over was heightened when the enemy switched to night bombing only to find that the Beaufighters were as capable of destroying the enemy aircraft at night as the Spitfires were doing during the day. Harry was involved in seeing that the Beaus were equipped with AI radar and remembers the Fighter Controller directing one such Beau towards a raider until its own radar took over.

I had time to dash from underground to witness the first ever sight (in Malta) of a successful radar directed attack. The huge orange fireball of the enemy plane exploding in the night sky was a fantastic sight.

While on Malta, Harry had made friends, as had many others, with a Maltese family. The mother had died but the eldest daughter, Julie Psiala, although still under 21, brought up the younger children and helped run a small bar. When Harry returned to Malta 33 years later, he went to look for the family, who were in the same house, although the bar was now a small grocery shop.

Imagine then, when I walked into the shop after all those years and simply asked the girl serving, 'Julie?', and the lady answered, 'Corporal Yorkie!' – my affectionate nickname in the war.

* * *

Owen Howell also arrived on the island in September 1941, courtesy of the RN cruiser, *HMS Euryalus*. Initially he helped to service the Blenheims at Luqa, where servicing was carried out in the open, as there were no hangars left. Like Harry, Owen was seeing the lull before the storm!

He was pleased to discover a pre-war friend whom he had worked with, who was now a sergeant Wireless Operator/Air Gunner on the Blenheim squadron. They met by chance when both sheltered by a wall during an air raid. They made a date to go out together, but that never happened. The friend did not return from a sortie on 6th February, 1942. (Three Blenheims of 21 Squadron were shot down on this date by Me 109s of JG53.)

At this time, Luqa was mainly the island's bomber station but the incessant rain flooded both Hal Far and Ta Kali, so Hurricanes were flown in from Ta Kali, adding to the airmens' work load. There were some occasional moments of relief, mostly concerning food.

> One could occasionally buy an egg sandwich on the black market, comprising an egg and two slices of Hobs – Maltese bread – but it cost nearly a whole day's pay. Chips fried on a little primus stove with the egg was more expensive, about five shillings. Olive oil and kerosene were both in terribly short supply and strictly rationed but even this rare treat had ceased by late in 1942. By then neither were available at any price!

Strangely the Gut continued to find food to sell and on their off days, the men would go there for a feed as much as for the Sherry Girls and other frolics. One of their dishes was a portion of boiled rice – 'solid like a cake' – delicious when one was hungry. The airmen also tended to spend at least a part of their day off visiting the many pals in Imtarfa Hospital. With so many casualties there was always someone there to visit.

As the siege and the bombing wore on a more serious medical condition began to take its toll. This was anxiety neurosis or to put it more plainly, men became 'bomb happy'. Men, like machines, have their limits. Just as an electric motor will seize or cease to function if persistently overloaded or denied maintenance, so also will a human being. It is a wonder in retrospect, that so many managed to carry on.

When Owen became part of a new maintenance team in April 1942, to help look after the Spitfires that were due to arrive, he was moved to Kirkop village by Safi Strip. Their laundry was done by the women of the village who turned out clean and beautifully ironed clothes, which was surprising as by then soap had become extremely scarce.

One of Owen's most ghastly moments came on one of his days off. He was in a dghaissa, a Maltese rowing boat, being ferried across from Sliema with two Maltese women and a priest as the other passengers.

> We were about half way across when the air raid started – the target being Grand Harbour. I have never felt so vulnerable. Bombs whistled down, diving aircraft, shrapnel falling all around us and sizzling as it hit the water. The women were screaming and 'Hail Mary's' came thick and fast from the priest.

On another occasion, Owen Howell and some mates were walking across the airfield from Luqa school in which they were billeted, to commence their daily tasks.

Without warning, six Me 109s came screaming across the runway, strafing and dropping 'butterfly' bombs directly on us as we hit the ground. How we escaped injury I shall never know.

Pilot Officer Philip Lewis had two attempts to reach Malta from the Middle East. During June 1942 he was one of several RAF men on board the *Potaro* in an Alexandria convoy, which was forced back by dive bombers. Later he was flown to the island.

As a defence expert his jobs varied enormously. On one occasion he had to organise contractors to get on with the job in hand, which was to dig a ditch across a waterlogged airfield to prevent flooding. Raids were heavy and it was necessary to 'persuade' the workers with the aid of a Tommy Gun! He was also part of the island's anti-invasion team. He had to train others in gas and fire drills. He was given a two pound pom-pom gun, salvaged from a sunken ship, which he mounted and helped to man, on the top of the caves near Ta Kali.

Lewis also had to see that each Station knew what to do if invasion forces appeared. This required practices. One practice proved to be almost too realistic. Since part of the drill was for a Station to demolish itself, this, during the practice, all but happened! Fortunately it was stopped just in time.

Lewis has several first hand accounts of meetings with the legendary Canadian fighter ace, 'Screwball' Beurling. As part of his duties, Lewis had to check through the accounts of the sergeant's mess, and one day while there, he encountered Beurling, who was still a sergeant pilot at that stage. He was writing a letter to his mother and Philip asked him if he was writing to tell her about the DFM he had just received. Beurling said, not, – 'Because she would think he was doing something dangerous!'

On another occasion Beurling was before Air Commodore W A B Bowen-Buscarlet for a commission which he hadn't applied for. He told the AOA that he didn't like saluting and that the hat which he was wearing wasn't his... 'But in the end they did commission him, in spite of his protests, when his score in Malta reached 22½!' – and – 'Beurling was always very particular about his cannon ammunition and was always upset if he didn't kill the enemy pilot!'

When Beurling was shot down and wounded in the heel, Phil Lewis went to visit him in hospital, and asked him what he would do after the war. 'Go to China,' Beurling had answered, 'there's always a war on there.'

One of Philip's more pleasant tasks was to visit nearby Gozo island once a month to see that the radar crew on this undefended island were all right. He would bring back eggs, bought for 2/6d each and a carboy of the potent Ambeet Gozo wine, which some called 'Stuka Juice'.

Another unusual recollection was when the Royal Engineers on Malta somehow made from virtually nothing, three iron lungs. Which helped greatly to combat the polio outbreak which threatened to sweep through the island where so many unhygienic habits had become commonplace due to lack of almost every kind of civilised commodity.

Because of his varied duties, Lewis was provided with a motor cycle which he could see would be extremely useful but he hadn't ridden one before. He was loathe to turn down such an offer so went off in secret to practise mounting and riding it.

There was also a truly tragic incident after he had managed to get hold of a bottle of brandy, which he was hoarding for a special occasion. He recalls:

> One night I was awakened by the Medical Officer who explained that a life raft with two of our airmen had been sighted in the Med and they thought that it would be a very nice gesture if they dropped some sustenance, including my precious brandy. After much heart searching, I agreed, but you can imagine what I said when I found out later that they were enemy aircrew!

James Ward arrived in Malta due to a not too unusual wartime posting cock-up! Having been accepted for aircrew, he was well on the way to completing his Wireless Operator/Air Gunner training when suddenly in September 1941 he received a surprise posting overseas. Assuming this was to some further training establishment, he went, lugging all his flying gear with him. He found himself on a merchant ship bound for Malta and upon his arrival was assigned to ground duties. When eventually he left Malta some years later, he was, sadly, no longer fit for aircrew duties – the months of bombing, food shortages, over work, stress and so on, having taken their toll.

So sure was he that he would eventually be able to continue with his flying training, he retained all the flying gear for over a year before finally returned it to stores, exchanging it for a slip of paper, leaving the building with a lump in his throat. What follows is James' story, told in his own words:

I arrived in Malta on the merchantman *Clan Ferguson*, one of an original convoy of 42 ships,[2] in September, 1941. As we entered the Med the captain called us together, warning us of the impending danger, explaining that, as we carried a cargo of high-octane aviation spirit and bombs, if we were unlucky enough to be hit, we were unlikely to know much about it! The convoy included the carrier *Ark Royal*, battleship *Nelson* and the cruiser *Kenya*.

The convoy took quite a battering, day and night, from dive bombers and U-boats, while covering the 1,000 miles from Gib to Malta, but despite the number of attacks, loss of life was comparatively light. As we finally disembarked in Grand Harbour, the air raid siren went – a sound we were to hear all too often during the ensuing years.

Despite my protests and pleas to be sent on the elusive air gunnery course I'd been expecting, I was sent to the Inter-Command W/T Station, deep underground at Lascaris, in Valletta. I was billeted at the Connaught Home in Floriana and once air raids increased, the daily walk between there and Valletta was sometimes quite frightening; there were times when I thought I wouldn't make it.

When things were really bad I would walk in the old railway tunnel for some of the way but this was not an easy choice. It would be full of Maltese, who would be praying, chanting and chattering away, all more or less at the same time. It was an eerie scene with the light cast by the candlelit shrines with a really stifling atmosphere; being a heady mixture of incense and sweat.

One night I had just turned in, hoping to get a few hours of badly needed sleep, when a stick of bombs straddled my

---

[2] Many must have stopped at Gibraltar. Ten only left for Malta - Operation Halberd. All arrived in Malta except for the *Imperial Star*. Several RN escorts were damaged.

billet. There was one hell of a bang and the force of the explosion shot me and several of my comrades, clean out of our beds. It was a miracle nobody was hurt, although the building was damaged.

We were also plagued with bedbugs, finding it impossible to get rid of them entirely. They were virtually invisible in the bed's springs and our body warmth activated them, so we were bitten during the night, resulting in irritating and quite painful sores. After trying without success to burn them out with matches, some bright spark hit on the idea of trying a blowlamp.

Although even this drastic measure didn't solve the problem, it did considerably reduce their numbers, and anyway, after a time we almost got used to them. In the spring of 1942 I was moved to the Vernon Club in Valletta.

My main job was the sending and receiving of messages, all in code, and ranging in priority from Important, Immediate, Most Immediate and Emergency. Accuracy was the prerequisite, particularly as the coded messages frequently contained vital operational information. Occasionally I would be in contact with the United Kingdom – times which had their own special poignancy, for as the weeks turned into months and the months into years, so it became more difficult to visualise that green and pleasant land I had left so long ago. Would I ever see it again?

Although the memory does play tricks, of one thing I am certain, and that is that I went almost two years without having a hot bath! Shaving was nearly always done with cold water and ordinary soap. I have no recollection of receiving either medical or dental treatment, apart from having one tooth removed. Flea and bug bites – even the odd dose of 'Malta Dog' – were not deemed to be sufficiently serious to merit the attention of the MO.

The bombing was always a problem, and three incidents had a marked effect on me, The first concerns Luqa. During the height of the bombing during 1942, parties from Signals were taken up to the aerodrome by lorry to help fill in bomb craters. There was no shortage of work because as soon as the old craters were filled with rubble, so fresh ones were made. This activity was undertaken in our off duty time, as we were doing a 12 hour on, 12 hour off Signals Watch!

We were only allowed to dash for cover when Luqa itself was about to be attacked. On one never to be forgotten occasion, with the temperature in the high 80's, as we were sweating away filling in craters, Luqa was attacked without warning, bombs falling uncomfortably close. As we dashed headlong for such cover as available – and there wasn't much – several Me 109s flew in low strafing. In our blind panic we could see bullets kicking up the dust just yards away. We flung ourselves behind a low wall, exhausted, very frightened but miraculously unhurt. There is little doubt their target was a number of aircraft dispersed about the airfield, rather than a collection of scurrying airmen, although that would be little consolation if one was unlucky enough to be hit.

The second incident concerns Lascaris. Maltese sentries maintained a round the clock guard duty at the entrance to the underground signals section and naturally we got to know the individual sentries quite well. Going on duty one afternoon, during an air raid on Valletta, I had just had a friendly word with the sentry on duty and was about halfway down to the Section, when there was one hell of a bang and a great 'whoosh'! I was almost knocked off my feet and later I heard that the sentry was killed and a large number of other people injured.

The third hairy experience was really brought about by carelessness on the part of three of us. 'Taffy' Williams and I, together with a third Signals comrade, decided to make use of an off duty spell by 'borrowing' some cycles and getting some much needed exercise. However, the siren went just as we were in the vicinity of the submarine pens, and we realised with some horror that the pens were the target, as the Stukas screamed down and all hell was let loose. With no time to run for cover, we simply dropped where we were, pulling the bikes on top of us – as some form of protection! We must have taken leave of our senses, for we hadn't even started out with our tin helmets![3] With bombs raining down and AA guns

---

[3] Somehow that terrible winter, the RAF all got hold of army tin helmets which we wore at all times as protection against shrapnel falling.

blazing away, it was absolute pandemonium, and all the while, pieces of shrapnel were thudding down around us. How we survived I'll never know; maybe it was because of all the prayers we offered up as never before – which we all readily admitted afterwards. It was some time before we were composed enough to ride the bikes back to Valletta.

I suppose I would call 1941 the 'lead in year', at least for me. 1942 – the George Cross year – was the year of merciless bombing, the siege and near starvation. It was also the year of many invasion scares. So we come to 1943, which I look back on as the calming down and rehabilitating year. Perhaps the high point of that year was the surrender of the Italian fleet in September and as it lay at anchor off the Island, row upon row of ships of all shapes and sizes, it really was a sight to behold.

Although we Signals Wallahs got on very well together most of the time, there were times when we tended to become bored with all male company. Catering for those seeking a very different kind of female company, were I believe certain Maltese ladies of easy virtue resident in 'The Gut'. I suppose it was only natural that I should feel the need of female company that much more, when the girl to whom I had become engaged shortly before my overseas posting, wrote to me, breaking off our engagement. It came as a great shock to me coming as it did, out of the blue. It came at a bad time, April 1942, with the bombing at its height and the siege conditions worsening.

However, if only I had known then that by the autumn of 1944, such a devastating experience was to prove a blessing in disguise, for it was in that October that I met Margaret, the love of my life, to whom I have now been happily married for over 40 years.

CHAPTER TWELVE

THE SPITFIRES WHICH SAVED MALTA

Much has been written about the Spitfires and how the arrival of this magnificent fighter aircraft in March to May 1942, eventually saved Malta from almost certain destruction. Worthier pens than mine, namely those of such writers as 'Laddie' Lucas, Tim Johnston, Ray Hesslyn and Lord James Douglas-Hamilton, have told this epic story and told it well.

Likewise, much has also been written about one particular Spitfire pilot, George Frederick Beurling, better known to the general public as 'Screwball' Beurling, who, alongside another pilot, Adrian Warburton, will always be remembered by those concerned with the offence and defence of Malta from the air.

First, however, we have to cover the background as to how Spitfires were initially assigned to the island for defensive purposes. It began in January 1942. Group Captain Basil Embry DSO DFC, Sector Commander at RAF Wittering in England, was asked by the C in C Fighter Command, Air Chief Marshal Sholto Douglas, to fly out to the Middle East and advise on fighter and bomber operations and tactics to the AOC of the Desert Air Force in Cairo. He went out, via Malta, in October 1941, and having completed that assignment, decided it might prove useful to drop in again on Malta to see if Hugh Pughe Lloyd needed any similar help. Lloyd, never a man to refuse help or advice, welcomed Embry who immediately set about learning all about Malta's fighter defences and tactics.

He arrived on Malta on 14 January 1942, spent some time in the island's central fighter operations buildings and then made the rounds of the various squadrons to talk to the pilots. After discussions with Lloyd, Embrey gave him a report he had compiled, which Lloyd found most helpful. The report read as follows:

SECRET AOC

As a result of my investigation into the Fighter defence of your command, I make the following recommendations.

AIRCRAFT.

1. It is quite clear that Hurricane II aircraft lack the necessary performance to deal with the interception problem at Malta. It appears that if a Hurricane Squadron is scrambled as soon as warning plots are received, ie: when the enemy aircraft cross the coast of Sicily, they can only attain a height of 15,000ft by the time the enemy have crossed the coast of Malta. Enemy fighters are, on many occasions, crossing the coast of Malta at a height of between 20–25,000ft. They therefore always have a big advantage over our fighters which makes it practically impossible for the Hurricane IIs to take on the Me 109s which are superior in performance in every respect to the Hurricanes. It follows that the Hurricanes cannot take on escorted enemy bombers without grave risk to themselves, as top cover cannot be provided. The answer to the problem is for three Spitfire V Squadrons to be made available as soon as possible. This type of aircraft should supply the answer, as they are capable of climbing to approximately 25,000ft in 15 to 20 minutes, thus enabling them to achieve a height advantage over the enemy fighters. If the enemy are not prepared to meet the Spitfires on equal terms as regards height it will mean that the bombers which they are escorting will be forced to fly at a greater height, and thereby reducing the accuracy and effectiveness of their bombing.

2. The enemy are carrying out most of their bombing with Ju 88s which are protected by heavy armour, therefore some form of cannon is required to deal with them, and I suggest that the ideal aeroplane would be the Kittyhawk, which is armed with four .5 cannons. This type of aircraft is in use in the Middle East and is likely to become available in greater numbers in the near future. A further advantage of using this type of aeroplane is that they could be supplied from the Middle East without difficulty as they could fly direct from the Benghazi area, provided they are fitted with long range tanks.

3. My recommendations are that the fighter force for Malta should be three Spitfire V and two Kittyhawk Squadrons. As an immediate measure I recommend that Middle East should be asked to make one Kittyhawk Squadron available

without delay. It should be borne in mind that Spitfires and Kittyhawks require good aerodromes for their operation and if possible they should be operated from runways.

4. The principle drawback to these types of aircraft is that they are not particularly suitable for operations at night, except in the hands of very skilled pilots. Consideration should, therefore, be given to the retention of one Hurricane II Squadron for use as a Night Fighting Unit. This should be equipped with Hurricane IICs as their armament (four 20 mm cannons) is particularly effective for this type of work.

EQUIPMENT

5. Scarcity of essential spares is adversely affecting serviceability: strong representation should be made to Middle East to bring about an improvement in this direction. I consider that a far higher establishment for spares is required here than in any other Command due to the difficulty of obtaining them rapidly.

GCI and RDF[1] INSTALLATION

6. This matter has already been discussed by us and requires no further comment by me, except so far as the GCI is concerned. I am of the opinion that immediate use could be made of the GCI set available on the island; although it may not be 100% efficient, a certain amount of useful information could be obtained by calibrating tubes for a limited range. I understand that until re-sited it will give no information over the island itself nor will it give long distance information, but accurate plots could be obtained of aircraft within a range belt of 20 to 5 miles distance. This information would be particularly useful when dealing with mine laying aircraft, or enemy reconnaissance aircraft which remain in the vicinity of the island for any length of time. My recommendation, therefore, is that the GCI set should be put into operation at once.

TRAINING

7. Immediate improvement could be brought about in the training of fighter pilots by paying more attention to air firing. The key to success in air fighting is accurate shooting and skill will only

[1] Ground Control Interception & Radio Direction Finding (Radar).

be obtained by constant practice in shooting at moving targets in the air. Steps should, therefore, be taken to make available at least two aircraft for drogue towing. Useful training can also be done by the use of clay pigeon shooting, if the equipment can be made available and hung in crew rooms.

MORALE

8. The morale of pilots seems to be high although the obsolescent Hurricane IIs are having a certain effect on the pilots. I am informed that German fighter pilots often fly in front of our Hurricanes and perform upward rolls and other manoeuvres in order to show off the superiority of the Me 109Fs. This is bound to have an increasingly adverse effect on the morale of our pilots. I therefore consider that every posssible step should be taken to make Spitfire Vs and Kittyhawks available with the least delay.

9. The retention of Squadrons at Malta for long periods is inadvisable as I am sure that constant flying over the sea and other administrative disadvantages which accrue from living in a cramped space affects the outlook of the fighter pilots. I therefore recommend that if possible, steps should be taken to change personnel at least every six months and, where possible, complete squadrons should be changed with Middle East every two or three months; this may not be possible with the Spitfire Squadrons, as it is probable that they will not be used in the Middle East for some time to come.

OPERATIONS FROM CONTROL

10. It appears to me that a stricter degree of control in the Operations Room is necessary. There is far too much talking and the resulting noise affects good control. It also occurred to me that there were too many spectators present. I recommend that no person should be allowed to enter the Operations Room without permission of a senior officer or the Senior Controller.

11. The method of control is not the same as used in Fighter Command, and I recommend that it should be changed. The pilots are being given a running commentary on what is happening, ie: 'Enemy approaching from NE at such and such a height' or 'Enemy aircraft are over a given point'. I recommend that definite instructions should be given to

pilots, ie: 'Enemy in your vicinity VECTOR 240 ANGELS 15,000'. I make this recommendation because I consider pilots have sufficient to think about in the air and it has been proved at home that definite instructions produce better results. Moreover, RT security is compromised. I understand that this method of control is not possible through lack of Fixer Stations, but a third station will be in use within the next few days. When it is working, 'PIPSQUEAK' should be used, and the method recommended above adopted.

12. Although the requirements of Malta may be somewhat different from other theatres of war, I would prefer to see centralised control by one Controller from the Operation Room instead of the aircraft being controlled by 'Jim Crows'. I feel it is far better to have all information passed to a central operations room and make one man responsible for controlling: he has the full picture before him, whereas, 'Jim Crows' only have a very limited picture.

CONTROLLERS

13. Although I do not wish to give a hasty opinion, I consider an improvement could be brought about by the introduction of a really experienced Controller who would improve the room organisation and standard of control. I recommend Squadron Leader DAKIN now serving in the Middle East; he should be given the rank of Wing Commander. Wing Commander Rabagliati has not the experience of Operations Room work to criticise or bring about an improvement in the organisation. He informs me that when he was serving in Fighter Command he spent his time at satellite aerodromes and, therefore, did not have the opportunity to gain Operations Room experience.

WING COMMANDER FLYING

14. I recommend that a Wing Commander Flying (Wg Cdr Rabagliati) be used more in the capacity of an itinerant Staff Officer rather than as a controller. He should exercise supervision over the training of all fighter Squadrons, fly with them periodically, and exercise general control over the Operations Room in the same way as a Sector Commander does at home. This should bring about an improvement in the practical side of control, the general standard of training, and the

co-ordination of the work of all fighter squadrons. He would also form a strong link between the fighter pilots and you.

R/T SECURITY

15. It appears to me that consideration is not being given to R/T security. For example, the broadcasting of the information referred to in para 11 above, if picked up by the enemy, could be made use of to his advantage and I believe that this may materially affect interceptions. I recommend that a wireless security officer from the Middle East should be asked to visit Malta and look into this subject. I am not aware if the enemy are making use of our W/T and R/T information but it is a well known fact that they do so in other commands, and I therefore consider that serious consideration should be given to this problem.

Basil Embry Group Captain

* * *

There are some who consider this report to be THE one which helped save Malta. Doubtless Lloyd did not object much to the contents for any help in getting better men and equipment would have been welcomed. Embry, being Embry, despite being a mere Group Captain, took the report right to the top and almost single handed saw to it that it be immediately implemented. None could deny those piercing blue eyes and grim determination.

Not everything recommended by the Group Captain could or would, be considered. One cannot imagine, for instance, Lloyd ordering aircraft to fly around the island – between raids – towing a drogue, while valuable ammunition was blasted into it by trainee fighter pilots! Nor, of course, were Kittyhawks ever used on Malta. However, some of the recommendations were acted upon. A senior fighter controller was appointed – Group Captain A B Woodall, or Woody as he was affectionately known – who had been a Controller in England and his experience proved a great asset over Malta.

The greatest thing, however, was that Spitfires were recommended and were soon on their way.

* * *

Rather than repeat, or attempt to make a summation of well told tales, the story of the Spitfires of Malta will here be covered in three quite distinct phases. First, the near disaster phase which covers the period from March to early May 1942. The second phase details the arrival of more Spitfires on the 9th May, 1942 while the third phase will include the period June to October 1942.

Phase one is really a sorry tale of poorly prepared aircraft arriving on the island in the hands of largely inexperienced pilots and consequently of the fighters being destroyed, both on the ground and in the air, in such large numbers that by the end of April their inability to master the Luftwaffe and its Messerschmitt 109s had cast a deep shadow over the whole island.

April 1942 was the month when the enemy bombing had reached its peak and also when the island's defences were at their lowest ebb. The March blitz had been heavy and everyone felt that only the arrival of Spitfires could save them. When they did arrive and were almost immediately written off in bombing, strafing or air combat, the disappointment was immense.

This first batch headed in for Malta after flying off the carrier *HMS Eagle* on 7th March, led by Squadron Leader S B Grant, who had flown in the Battle of Britain. In all 15 Spitfires, led in by four Blenheims,[2] landed at Ta Kali. On the 10th the Spitfires were ready for action and in a mid-morning clash, Flight Lieutenant Philip 'Pip' Heppell DFC shot down a 109 of JG53, while other pilots claimed hits on three more. Later that day, came the first Spitfire loss, JG53 gaining its revenge by shooting down Pilot Officer Ken Murray, who baled out although his parachute failed to deploy properly and he died of his injuries that same evening. While searching for Murray, another Spitfire was damaged, its pilot wounded. Over the next few days, other Spitfires were either lost (four shot down and two destroyed on the ground) or damaged, but soon a second batch arrived from *HMS Eagle* on the 21st, led by another Battle of Britain veteran, Squadron Leader E J 'Jumbo' Gracie DFC. There should have been 16 of them but only nine arrived as a Blenheim which should have navigated the other seven to Malta, failed to arrive. The new arrivals joined the others. There were now two Spitfire squadrons, 249, which had formed when the

---

[2] The Blenheims did not fly off the carriers. They came from Gibraltar to intercept, navigate and lead.

first batch arrived, and now 126, both of which having been earlier equipped with Hurricanes. However both units had to operate, at this stage, with both types of fighter; depending on serviceability.

The seven other Spitfires eventually arrived on the 29 March, *Eagle* again making a foray into the central Mediterranean. Four of the new pilots were Canadians, and were led by Flight Lieutenant A R H 'Butch' Barton DFC, yet another Battle of Britain veteran. The island's Spitfires fought on over the next weeks but being so few in number, they were only used in twos or fours. Losses, damage and lack of spares meant that they could never be used in force, but they scored steadily while their Hurricane companions continued to inflict damage on the raiders.

It was obvious that more Spitfires were needed, and in larger numbers. These came in April, in the form of not one but two new Squadrons, 601 and 603. In all 47 Spitfires, led by jumbo Gracie, the units being commanded by Squadron Leaders J D Bisdee DFC and Lord D Douglas-Hamilton, took off from the US carrier *Wasp* on 20th April. All but one landed on Malta; the 47th had headed south for Africa, the pilot – an American – having confided to a pal that he had no intention of going to Malta. 601 went to Luqa, 603 to Ta Kali. It had been intended that some of the new arrivals would go to reinforce 126 and 249 Squadrons but things didn't turn out like that.

The Luftwaffe, all too aware of the new arrivals, made a determined effort to destroy them by attacking all three fighter airfields during the rest of the day. Some Spitfires were lost and others damaged, while still more were reported unserviceable, so that by the morning of the 21st, only 27 Spitfires were available. After another day of hectic fighting, this number was reduced to just 17 by the morning of the 22nd! By the 27th the total fighter force of the island was so reduced (although not all the aircraft had been destroyed) that little actual resistance could be mounted. By the end of the month just seven Spitfires and a few Hurricanes were all that were serviceable. During April at least 22 Spitfires and 19 Hurricanes had been destroyed on the ground; with others lost in combat.

But more Spitfires were on their way. The US carrier *Wasp* and the British *HMS Eagle* were on their way again in early May, thanks to the personal intervention of Winston Churchill who asked his friend President Roosevelt to borrow once more the American carrier. This time however, the Spitfires were in far better condition and 64 headed for Malta off the carriers' decks on 9th May 1942. They were led to the island by four of Malta's veteran air fighters who had flown to Gibraltar for the occasion – Stan Grant, Ron West, 'Laddie' Lucas and Buck McNair. Of the 64, two failed to arrive and one crashed as it took off, while another was forced to land back on the *Wasp* due to a technical fault. This latter feat was quite extraordinary, for none of the pilots had been trained to land back on a carrier deck; nor did the aircraft have a hook to catch the arresting wires.

Things on Malta were very different this time. Lloyd had things organised down to a fine art and every effort was made to put the arriving fighters into full trim and getting them off the ground, armed and refuelled and back into action swiftly with an experienced Malta fighter pilot in control.

For each arriving Spitfire, a special dispersal pen had been prepared and numbered. Each pen contained a key maintenance man, an armourer to load the guns (the incoming fighter had only a small amount of ammo, purely for self defence – if this was not avoidable), a fitter to remove the overload fuel tanks and a refuelling team – often army men. As each fighter taxied off the runway area, an airman would guide the pilot straight to its pen where immediately it would be dealt with so it could, if required, be airborne and in fighting order in the absolute minimum time. By this time, Malta had acquired a sufficient number of highly experienced Spitfire pilots for one to be assigned to each pen.

The tired incoming pilot, virtually all of whom would have no Malta experience or even no operational experience of any kind, would, on arrival, hand over his Spitfire (in reality, he was almost literally turfed out and told to take cover or get lost!) to the Malta pilot waiting to receive it. The drill was rehearsed over and over again, so well in fact that in some cases, the Spitfire was ready for action within nine minutes.

The Germans knew only too well when the Spitfires would be expected to arrive. The carriers had to pass Gibraltar, where of course, enemy spies and agents would have little difficulty in finding out what was happening. The result is history.

So brilliant was the drill in the fighter pens, that when the Me 109s were on their way from their Sicilian airfields, they were met in the air by a number of Spitfires, brilliantly directed by, as usual, 'Woody'

– the imperturbable Group Captain A B Woodall, chief controller. A fierce air battle commenced, but this time the tables had been turned.

Woody's air controlling was always masterly. He would position the Spitfires at height south of the island. From there, with the sun behind them, they dived on the invaders coming in from the north, catching many before they even reached the airfields. The RAF pilots, with very few losses to themselves, destroyed on 9 May a considerable number of approaching enemy fighters and bombers but the real battle took place the next day.

Everything that the island possessed in the way of defences was thrown into this one, all important, almost desperate battle. The fast (38 kts) minelayer *HMS Welshman* (she had been disguised to look like a neutral French destroyer of the Leopold Class, having a French flag flying and with sailors topside dressed in distinctive French naval uniforms) had reached Malta after a furious dash from Gibraltar, at first light on the 9th and was swiftly unloaded. She had been converted into an emergency freight carrier. The *Welshman* carried, amongst other things, fresh supplies of ammunition for the island's AA gunners. These gunners, so long restricted in the number of rounds they could fire each day, suddenly had unlimited amounts of ammo to blast off whenever they saw an approaching armada of enemy aircraft. To protect itself, the *Welshman* had also brought in smoke generators which were immediately lit. In no time, Grand Harbour was completely covered with thick smoke. This enabled her to be swiftly unloaded without being damaged in any way by the raiders as well as giving the harbour a modicum of security.

A great number of AA guns had been moved around the harbour, so when the hostile aircraft did approach, they were met with such a carefully controlled box barrage that it was necessary for them to dive through a hail of flak, even to attack the general area where the ship lay.

Only 36 hours after the first Spitfires had arrived, the fighting which had occurred on the 9th and 10th, had completely changed the situation over Malta. Air superiority from the Luftwaffe had been wrested and it remained that way for the whole of the rest of the war over the island.

By the start of the second day, the 10th, virtually all the newly arrived Spitfires were still in first class fighting order and the fighter pilots, with their victories of the previous day still fresh upon them, were ready for further action. This time the Luftwaffe tried to approach in even greater numbers and a glorious air battle went on for most of that Sunday. It is not known for certain how many enemy aircraft were shot down on the 10th, but as many as 63 were claimed as destroyed or damaged, although only about 25 were claimed as certainties. It is significant that Rome Radio – notorious for grossly exaggerated claims, admitted that evening, the loss of 38 Axis aircraft, so obviously the actual losses were much higher. The accuracy of Rome Radio can be judged by the fact that it also claimed that in the course of the air battles during the day, no fewer than 47 Spitfires had been accounted for! In reality, the RAF lost just three with two pilots having safely landed by parachute.

Corporal Cyril Woods, an airman who wrote brilliantly about Malta, describes the day thus

> What a day it was! Barnum and Bailey and the Flo Ziegfield Follies had nothing on the show we saw that sunny day, the 10th of May. Stukas diving, Spitfires circling above the box barrage and picking them off as they flew clear. Ju 88s bombing from higher level. Eager Spitfire pilots chasing bombers right through the barrage, not always coming out whole. The sea from Malta to Italy looked like Henley Regatta, there were so many German crews in their dinghies with rescue launches picking them up.

The reaction of the Maltese and the Allied servicemen was instantaneous. Somehow everyone on the island sensed that the tables were now being turned. Many left the shelters in which they had lived for so long, to stand and cheer out in the open as the Spitfires tore into the German and Italian aircraft. It was all in the master plan in which the Navy and Army had a major part to play as well as the Air Force. 'Jumbo' Gracie had a lot to do with it; certainly Hugh Pughe Lloyd had a lot to do with it – and without doubt Woody Woodall controlled the air battle with his customary mastery.

Malta breathed again. A definite light at the end of the long dark tunnel could be seen. Morale was on the increase. Malta was in business again – as Rommel and his armies were about to discover.

Thus ended the second phase of the Spitfire's Malta battle.

* * *

The third phase followed soon after. Shortly after these May battles the bulk of the Luftwaffe was withdrawn from Sicily. Not because of the losses sustained but because Kesselring had already arranged for it in April. As commander of all German forces in the Mediterranean, it seemed obvious to him that Malta had been bombed to a standstill. His aircrews had been complaining that there were no more military targets to bomb and, as more aircraft were needed in the North African fighting, he had already arranged for much of his air arm to leave Sicily. Thus the air fighting over Malta after this early May period, slackened considerably.

However, as soon as it was obvious to the Allied war leaders that air superiority had been regained, they immediately started to re-introduce into the island the bomber and torpedo planes with which to harry Axis shipping. This was just as well because May and June were triumphant months for Rommel in the desert. He captured Tobruk and his Afrika Korps was now just 60 miles from Alexandria. All that he needed now was to stock up with men, fuel and ammunition so as to make a final push towards the Suez Canal and the oil fields of Arabia.

More Spitfires arrived on Malta. 17 on 19 May, 27 more on 3 June, 32 on 9 June, 31 on the 15 July with another 28 on the 21st. Most came off the decks of the *Eagle*, but all by RN carriers.

The air raids continued but many were now night raids rather than by day. Another important difference was that many were by Italian rather than German aircraft. The German fighter and bomber pilots were at all times exceedingly brave and, almost without exception, they attacked only military targets. The Italians, on the other hand, were utterly unpredictable. Quite a large number had no intention of risking their necks on Malta raids. It was a strange sight to see a whole formation of Italian bombers, escorted by Italian fighters, come near Malta only to drop their bombs into the sea as soon as the Hurricanes and Spitfires appeared, turn tail and head back to Sicily. We would then listen to Rome Radio making the most fantastic claims about the damage that they had achieved during those particular raids. They once claimed to have destroyed the railway marshalling yards in Valletta – a strange claim since Malta had no railway!

On the other hand, some Italian aircrew were almost foolishly brave. They would appear, always flying high, in tight formation as if giving an exhibition display at a public air show. They would fly across the island completely ignoring everything being fired at them both by guns and fighters. They would not break formation no matter what was happening. One by one, the wing men would be picked off but the other just flew on. What is more, some of their high level bombing was extremely accurate. However, these were the exceptions. For the most part, the Italians bombed the sea.

By as early as June, and certainly by July, Malta was once again on the offensive with aircraft and submarines operating afresh, destroying the supply ships which Rommel so desperately needed. Beauforts, Baltimores and Wellingtons had arrived and were causing havoc at sea. Beaufighters began to operate out of Ta Kali while the FAA's Swordfish and Albacores were once more in evidence from Hal Far. So while Kesselring had been correct in sending his aircraft to North Africa, in doing so he had allowed the RAF and FAA, as well as HM submarines, to operate again from Malta. Not surprisingly large sections of the Luftwaffe were returned to Sicily in order to try to regain air superiority over Malta and so destroy the offensive aircraft. This was the period when George Frederick Beurling, the greatest of all Allied fighter pilots to see action over Malta, appeared on the scene.

Beurling was then only a Sergeant pilot. He had operated in the UK before going to Malta so had some experience – and two air combat victories – but he had gained a bad reputation. He was an undisciplined and unruly individual who did not get on with either his brother pilots or his superiors. He had failed to be a part of the essential teamwork so necessary by the midwar years when flying sorties over France and Holland. Once over hostile territory he simply went off on his own. Even fighting in the desert sky needed teamwork, but there was perhaps one place where the individual might still shine – Malta.

So he, and others, now saw the beginning of the third phase of the Spitfire's air war over Malta. The Luftwaffe made its last desperate attempt to overcome the defenders and to neutralise the island by bombing, but this 'unsinkable aircraft carrier' in the Med just could not be blasted into submission. Only an airborne invasion would have succeeded, and the Germans had suffered too many losses in its airborne operations, when capturing nearby Crete in 1941, that they never really considered this as a serious, although obvious, option.

* * *

George 'Screwball' Beurling was one of the arrivals from the *Eagle* on 9 June, being assigned to 249 Squadron. At first he made no marked impression on the air battle, largely due to enemy activity being then mostly confined to night raids. The Canadian had arrived with a rather unsavoury reputation as an unruly, undisciplined pilot. One who was likely to break out of formation and go off on his own, was not popular. That he was a good pilot with exceptional eyesight was however acknowledged by all.

It is worth going into Beurling's history as it is quite remarkable. A Canadian of Swedish descent, his father was a commercial artist. From a very early age, George had been bitten with the urge to fly and he saved every penny he had for flying lessons. In fact he qualified as a pilot when aged 14 although too young to hold an actual licence. Nevertheless he flew whenever his finances enabled him to do so.

Once an operational fighter pilot on Malta, he became as thorough a killer as anyone in WWII. He was a fanatic about Good and Evil and never showed any understanding of the grey areas in between. He invariably carried a small Bible with him in the air; one which his mother had given to him. He was extremely fond of his mother, writing home to her constantly, but made no mention of his combats so as not to worry or alarm her. So, although he carried a Bible, it was fairly clear from his actions that what intrigued him was the Old Testament vengeance rather than the New Testament 'turning the other cheek!'

Almost as soon as he could fly he did his level best to get into an air war – any air war! He regarded the Japanese as Evil and the Chinese as Good, so consequently tried to enlist in the Chinese Air Force in 1937 in order to fight the Japanese in China, but failed. Two years later he was trying to join the Finns in their fight with Russia. When that failed he found himself a passage to England in 1940, jumped ship, reported to the nearest British recruitment office where he announced he had come to fight with the RAF against Germany.

He failed to bring any proof of education, of being a pilot, not even his birth certificate, so was rejected. Undaunted, he took passage on a ship again, returned to Canada, collected the required documents, and once again on the same ship, returned to England. Now accepted, he trained as a pilot and finally received a posting to No 403 RCAF Squadron.

With exceptional shooting ability and his equally exceptional eyesight – he would spend hours trying to pick out tiny objects at great distances – he might well have proved a good fighter leader, but being almost completely undisciplined, would simply break away from his squadron and attack enemy aircraft on his own. That he shot down at least two FW 190 fighters was no justification for this behaviour and he soon became very unpopular. No wonder that he was sent to Malta. When UK squadrons had to furnish a pilot for this overseas duty, they were more than pleased to have got rid of him: as earlier also had been the case of Adrian Warburton!

In many respects, Malta needed, and also forged, individualists and Beurling, like Warburton before him, easily made the grade. In WW II, Malta, for the likes of men such as Beurling, was 'a fighter pilot's paradise'.

With his phenomenal eyesight he was invariably the first of any formation to spot the incoming enemy raiders and by this time, he flew a Spitfire so naturally that it seemed a part of him. His knowledge of air tactics too was above the average. No sooner had he spotted his prey than he was positioning himself for a surprise attack. He never fired at random and never fired to just damage a plane. He fired to shoot it down; to hit and kill the enemy pilot. He would withhold his fire until he was at remarkably close range and in consequence, shot down aircraft after aircraft while using an almost absurdly low amounts of ammunition. In a period of six days he shot down ten of the enemy – all fighters – and received the DFM.

Much of the credit of his success must go to his Flight Commander – later his Squadron Commander – P B 'Laddie' Lucas DFC. Lucas could see he would never change Beurling, so decided to use the man's natural attributes to advantage. Laddie took him to one side, told him to trust him and that he would give him ample opportunities to shoot down enemy aircraft but, at the same time, warned the Canadian that if he abused that trust, he would post him off the island. Like Warburton, Beurling would do anything for the rare individual whom he was prepared personally to respect. After that, Laddie Lucas never had the smallest trouble with him – except his scruffy appearance – but he could put up with that considering the man's results!

Within a week of receiving his DFM, Beurling shot down another six or eight aircraft, to receive a bar to his DFM. His claims were always extremely honest. He just didn't say, 'I have shot down a Messerschmitt 109 or a Macchi 202,' he would describe where his bullets had gone. On those few occasions when it was possible to check the results from the wreckage of his victims which fell on the island, the bullets were exactly where he said they were. Beurling had few Probables or Damaged in his score. He shot to kill.

Beurling neither smoked nor drank, nor had anything to do with girls, believing that all three might have an adverse effect upon his eyesight or his ability. In appearance he was rough and ready but he had quite a sensitive thick lower lip. It was obvious from the adroit way he handled a Spitfire that he had a beautiful 'pair of hands'; inherited from his artistic father perhaps?

As his score mounted it was clearly impossible to continue awarding bars to his DFM so it was suggested he take a commission, which George flatly refused, seeing no point in being an officer, especially as he generally had no respect for officers – except Laddie Lucas – and did not want responsibility. But in the end he was just commissioned and that was that – almost a unique turn of events in RAF history! However, it is believed that Laddie was able to talk him round to accepting the situation and wearing the rank that went with it.

In almost no time at all Beurling's score was way beyond that of any pilot on Malta, some of whom had been fighting there for much longer. His final score over the island amounted to 8 Mc 202s, 15 Me 109s, a couple of Ju 88s with another shared and an Italian Re 2001 fighter, making a total of 26 and a third. With his two earlier kills his grand total was 28 1/3, one Probable (109) and four Damaged (three 109s and a Cant). All achieved between June and October 1942 and despite him going down with a bout of 'Malta Dog' in August and September; all while the Malta blitz was not at its height! He also received the DFC and then the DSO.

Finally, on 14 October, Beurling made his final claims over Malta – a Ju 88 and two Me 109s but, in going to the aid of another pilot, was himself hit and wounded in the heel and arm. With his Spitfire badly damaged, he had to take to his parachute. Rescued from the sea, he was sent back to England in a Liberator, which crashed en route at Gibraltar. Beurling broke a leg but survived although a number of people died in the crash.

Recovering in England, he flew ops again in late 1944 over Europe, adding three FW 190s to his score, but enemy aircraft were then few and far between and the Malta days were long past.

Beurling was destined to die in a plane crash outside Rome in

Ju 88 bombers on Sicily, preparing for a raid in Malta 1942. This fast bomber could almost outrun the worn out Hurricanes. *E C P Armes*

Loading flares into a Special Flight Wellington. *Imperial War Museum*

American pilot RAF, RN and Army men refuel and re-arm a Spitfire in Malta. Note the anti-blast wall in the top picture, built from empty 4 gallon petrol tins filled with rubble.

Me 109 crash-landed in Malta. The pilot Gunther Hannak from I/JG77 was taken prisoner May 5th 1943. He claimed to have shot down a total of 12 aircraft over Malta. *Eric Hughes*

During the bombing fires seldom broke out on Malta due to the stone buildings. Occasionally a fuel or bomb dump (as here) was hit.

The George Cross Island Association, composed of ex-veterans of Malta, meets in Malta for a 1990 reunion. Fred Plenty, with stick, is the founder, Bill Looker (also ex-RN), the Chairman is next to him, with Tony Spooner on his other side. 20th March 1990. *Joe Crawshaw*

1948, flying supplies to Israel – another war where he obviously identified Good and Evil in conflict.

* * *

In concentrating upon the feats of Beurling over Malta, it has to be remembered that this was a period when the Spitfires of 185, 249, 603 and other squadrons, stayed on top. The two principal Ta Kali Spitfire Squadrons were 249 and 603. Between them in the months of May to October, they shot down several hundred hostile aircraft. Between 11–19 October alone, 131 enemy aircraft were claimed shot down at a cost of 34 Spitfires.

Some idea of the success of the Malta Spitfires can be judged by the fact that these successful aeroplanes, operating in the island's defence, produced two of the three top scoring Canadian pilots of the whole war – namely Beurling and H W 'Wally' McLeod DFC (12 over Malta, 20 overall during the war); also one of the top Americans, Claude Weaver DFM (10½ over Malta, 12½ overall); top Rhodesian, Johnny Plagis DFC (11 over Malta, 15 overall), three of the top Australians, A P Goldsmith DFC DFM (12 over Malta, 16 overall), 'Slim' Yarra DFM (12 over Malta) and Paul Brennan DFC DFM (10 over Malta); one of the top New Zealanders, Ray Hesslyn DFM (12 over Malta, 12½ overall), while Pat Schade DFM, who was born in Malaya scored 12 victories over Malta. Of the British pilots, Peter Nash DFC, Norman McQueen DFC, Bill Rolls DFC DFM, and Mike Stephens DSO DFC all did well. These alone accounted for over 150 aircraft destroyed during a few months. 249 Squadron, at the war's end, had the highest score of any in the RAF.

Before Malta's war was to come to an end, over 1,000 air victories over Axis forces had been claimed, plus another 200 at least brought down by Ack-Ack gunners. This compares quite well with the figures for the Battle of Britain. It is now known that about 1,800 German aircraft were destroyed in that Battle, although the period of time was much smaller.

Thanks to the Spitfires, air superiority over Malta was regained and held. Almost immediately thereafter, torpedo and bomber aircraft were brought to the island and once again Rommel found his supply lines to Africa being severely disrupted. This same superiority enabled a few more ships to get through to the island. The August 1942 convoy, where 14 ships set out on Operation Pedestal, resulted in four cargo ships arriving – two damaged and the famous tanker Ohio bringing in oil supplies although her decks were almost awash after sustaining three or four damaging hits.

Victory over the supply lines to Rommel, assured victory in the desert for Montgomery's Armies during, and after, Alamein. This was followed in November by Operation Torch, the combined British and American landings in French North Africa, towards the western end of the Mediterranean. Later, with the Mediterranean more or less under Allied control, Malta became the spring board for the invasion of Sicily, Italy and finally the 'soft underbelly of Europe' – Southern France.

The small island, which in 1940 had been defended by just a handful of Gloster Gladiators had, on the eve of the invasion of Sicily in 1943, over 400 Spitfires on its fighter airfields, ready to form an umbrella over the ships that were launching the invading troops onto the enemy beaches. By that time, Malta's three airfields had expanded to six. Safi Strip had been turned into an airfield, a new airfield was built at Qrendi and the Americans, in a miraculous few weeks, had built yet another on Gozo.

As the Duke of Wellington was reported to have said at the time of Waterloo, it had been – 'A damned close run thing'. The Maltese are right to refer to the 10 May, 1942 as 'the glorious 10th of May'. The air victories won by the fighter pilots that day, turned the tide and, in effect, changed the whole face of the war in the Mediterranean. As in Britain in 1940, so in Malta in 1942, the Spitfires had served the Allies well and won more battle honours.

Before leaving the Spitfire story, mention must be made of the valuable work carried out by a few Spitfires equipped with cameras rather than guns. They carried out numerous Photographic Reconnaissance sorties under extreme difficulties. These enabled Malta to be kept aware of what the enemy strength was, what they were planning to do, and especially when they were planning to attempt their next convoy run to North Africa.

Four pilots were outstanding, and, as before, three of these were only in Malta because they had had to land there to refuel whilst ferrying PR aircraft to the Middle East! Not for the first – or last –

time, Hugh Pughe Lloyd was quick to appreciate their worth to Malta and to see that they got no further.

Harry Coldbeck was a New Zealander. It is not thought that he had ever before undertaken PR work but during the vital spring and summer of 1942, when the island was under its most ferocious attacks, he carried out more than 100 invaluable PR sorties. Few DFCs were more deservedly awarded.

He was joined by Sergeants Les Colquhoun and Dalley. Les also carried out a great number of equally meritorious and dangerous sorties in unarmed Spits. Les, unlike Harry, who was shot down in November 1942 and taken prisoner, went from strength to strength, both in Malta, UK, and then post war, as a test pilot with Vickers, ending up with wartime DFC and DFM and a peacetime George Medal. Dalley also served well.

There were many times during the worst of the bombing of 1942 when these two were almost the only pilots operating from Malta. It is surprising that their PR Spitfires remained undamaged on the ground as well as in the air. Both were incorporated into 69 Squadron, Harry being made a flight commander.

The third PR Spitfire pilot, of course, was Adrian Warburton, who had arrived back on the island in August 1942. It was for his astonishing 'nought feet' photographs of the coastal defences of the island of Pantellaria, prior to the capture of that island, that the Americans awarded Warby their DFC. For his equally amazing low level pictures of ALL the beach defences of Sicily, General Alexander personally thanked him. The General's signal included: 'They were technically perfect and complete as if taken on a peacetime exercise... extremely useful to the planning staffs and to the assaulting troops to whom they have been distributed.' Air Marshal Arthur Coningham sent a similar signal of congratulations, also mentioning Warburton by name. It was probably then that Air Marshal Tedder, AOC Middle East, described Warburton as: 'The most valuable pilot in the RAF.'

Malta had at all times to know what the enemy, so close at hand, were up to. The PR aircraft, in the sure hands of Coldbeck, Colquhoun, Warburton and Dalley, supplied the information regardless of both the enemy's superior air strength over their territories and of the appalling living conditions on the ground. Other notable 69 Squadron pilots included: Bloxam, Drew, Burges,

Durbridge, the Canadians, 'Mac' Brown and Ed Maloney, Lowery (NZ) and the Australian, Harry Smith. They were the eyes; the bombers and torpedo planes, the punch; the Spitfires, Hurricanes and night fighting Beaus, the guard. Together they wrote history.

CHAPTER THIRTEEN

THE MALTA SPECIAL OPERATIONS

Malta had its share of sinister air operations. In one way it was much easier for 'Special Flights' to be carried out from Malta. The island's respective AOCs, whether Sammy Maynard, Hugh Pughe Lloyd or later Keith Park, never had a massive Whitehall establishment overlooking their every action. If a unit commander thought up a new idea, he simply took it in person to the AOC. In most cases, if it seemed feasible, he simply said, 'Why not – let's give it a try!'

To jump ahead a bit, when I became fairly adept at locating enemy ships at night with my special ASV equipped Wellington, it irked me that there was not readily on hand, a warship or attacking aircraft with which to destroy the 'prize' which I and my crew had found, especially if that ship was 100 or so miles from Malta. In those circumstances, there was inadequate time to arrange for even an aircraft to fly and hit the enemy before dawn.

However, it came to my ears that 38 Squadron based near Cairo, had successfully modified some of their Wellingtons to carry torpedoes. Consequently I proposed that one of these aircraft be flown to Malta in order to operate alongside an ASV Wellington; together they might prove deadly.

As a rule it generally took me and my crew many hours of patient searching at night to locate an enemy ship or convoy. Therefore we flew with a maximum load of petrol as well as up to 60 large parachute flares, in the Wellington's bomb bays, instead of bombs. We carried two additional 140 gallon overload fuel tanks which in all gave us almost 12 hours endurance. If searching for a known ship which was thought to be much nearer Malta, we would carry less fuel but some 250 lb bombs with which to bomb it: as when we bombed and hit the Italian merchant ship *Amsterdam* of nearly 9,000 tons: skip bombing at night.

Since no Wellington could uplift both this extra fuel, flares and sometimes bombs, it was clearly impossible for the torpedo carrying Wimpy to accompany the ASV aircraft for hour upon hour, as it only carried the normal fuel load. The plan was that we would set out at last light and begin the long search, while the 38 Squadron aeroplane, 'torpedoed-up', would wait at Luqa at immediate readiness. If we were successful in locating a target, a message would be sent back but with a position, not of the target ship but one which was 50 miles away, on the Malta side of the target. We would then fly to that spot and when it was calculated that the torpedo plane should be arriving, we would drop flares and turn on our lights in order to attract it's pilot. Once together, we would fly in loose formation back to where the ship should now be.

Once we had relocated the ship, and with the ASV on a calm night we could detect even a single vessel at a range of 20 miles or so, I would fly straight at it and only pull away from the torpedo Wimpy when about a mile from it. It was reckoned that the torpedo aircraft should then be able to pick up the ship's wake and attack. A calm night with a moon was best as a ship's wake could then be seen at a considerable distance.

All went as planned on the actual operation. My crew and I located a suitable target, passed back the '50 mile away' position to Malta and the torpedo Wimpy headed out. Right on cue, we met up with it as we circled, lights blazing, although the moonlight was becoming progressively less bright.

Our plan continued to function with almost uncanny precision, for we relocated the ship on ASV and led in the other Wimpy. At about two miles away, I waggled our wings and turned aside and waited, expecting soon to see a mighty explosion. I saw nothing.

We were somewhere between Benghazi and Greece, 200 miles or so south east of Malta, and already we had been airborne for about 8 hours. With fuel soon to become a problem, I headed for home, to find that the torpedo plane had not sighted the ship in the increasingly darkening sky of the supposedly bright moonlight night!

Depressed at the failure of the operation at the very last hurdle, it was clear that the problem was due to the moonlight not giving sufficient illumination for the attack, but by then we had lost contact with the torpedo Wellington. Its crew, not being a bit enamoured with the appalling living conditions on Malta, now flew back to Egypt.

I still wonder if the crew of the torpedo Wellington discovered, as I did, that on that night as we met over the vast emptiness of the Central Mediterranean, there so happened to be a total eclipse of the moon! We had obviously not covered every possible eventuality when putting a completely novel idea in operation. But who would ever have thought of consulting an Almanac?

* * *

The first special air operation from Malta known to me, involved the faithful 'Stringbags' of 830 Squadron, FAA. In Sicily the Allies had a secret agent with a wireless set. The information he passed about enemy movements were valuable but he needed to be encouraged by money: quite a lot of money and not infrequently. Thus a Swordfish would, on dark nights, drop money in bags to him at a location on the slopes of Mount Etna. When the slow Swordfish became too vulnerable for these dangerous missions, a black painted Hurricane, flown by Flight Lieutenant Innes Westmacott, continued with this exacting job until the agent was rumbled and caught.

The Swordfish of 830 Squadron were also used for another important series of clandestine operations. Charles Lamb was the pilot as related in an earlier chapter, before he was captured. Other crew also dropped agents along the North African coast but due to the range of the aeroplane, they would be obliged to land on a lonely stretch of enemy road to refuel, before taking off again. This would be from four gallon cans of petrol which would be carried on board for this purpose. The skill and courage of the Fleet Air Arm pilots carrying out these hazardous operations was truly outstanding.

Another early special operation was to have profound consequences during the rest of the war. However, this was not one 'dreamed up' by anyone on Malta.

The British, by February, 1941, were beginning to think about how Europe might one day be reclaimed from the Nazi war machine. Under the code name Operation Colossus it was decided to test the effectiveness of dropping armed parachutists into occupied territory for sabotage purposes. The venue chosen was Southern Italy where, it was rightly considered, the enemy would not be too wide awake or well prepared. The actual target chosen was an aqueduct which, it was thought, carried most of the water required for a number of industrial concerns in the Campagna region.

No 78 Squadron, operating twin engined Whitley bombers, was chosen as this type could carry several extra men in its commodious fuselage. A force of about 40 men from the Royal Welsh Fusiliers were trained for the operation and the complete force, under Major T A G Pritchard, was flown to Malta in eight bombers. The party included at least one Italian, a man who had been a waiter at the Savoy Hotel in London but whose sympathies were with the Allies. He was chosen as he knew the dropping zone well.

Prior to the actual operation, Warburton, in a 69 Squadron Maryland, had taken a number of photographs, literally at ground level, of the aqueduct, to help in the planning. After completing their mission, it was intended that the Fusiliers would make for the coast and be picked up by a British submarine and returned to Malta. To create a diversion, four of the Whitleys would attack an airfield not too far distant, while the 40 men were crowded into the other four aircraft.

At first the plan went well. The men landed during the night of 10/11 February. They located the aqueduct, placed their explosives which they detonated successfully. However, the aqueduct, possibly soundly built by the Romans some 2,000 years previously, resisted the blasts and did not collapse. Frustrated, the men then blew up a nearby railway bridge before heading for their rendezvous off the coast in the Gulf of Salerno.

However, it had been snowing and their tracks led to their discovery. Also, one Whitley crashed close enough to arouse suspicion. As a result, the submarine *HMS Triumph* was ordered back to Malta once it was realised that the paratroops were likely to be apprehended. All were soon captured and the brave Italian waiter was shot as a spy.

An interesting aspect of this operation was that the young leader of the Whitley aircraft was Squadron Leader Willie Tait and he received a well deserved DSO. By the war's end, Tait had received the DSO and three bars! He had also led the raid on the German battleship *Tirpitz* which caused it to capsize in Trondheim Fjord, in 1944; thereafter being known as 'Tirpitz' Tait.

Despite the failure of the mission, it was considered that the idea was sound and lessons were learned and digested. Arising from this first drop of armed troops behind the enemy lines, subsequent raids were mounted by Commandos, the SAS, SOE agents, and so on.

Some months later, another Whitley arrived in Malta under the command of Flying Officer John Austin. This, too, was painted black and based at Luqa, though few knew why it was in Malta. It operated solely at night, departing and returning from operations which were shrouded in secrecy.

John Austin's difficult job was to drop canisters, loaded with gold, jewels and large US or UK currency notes, to the Jugoslav patriot fighters who were gallantly fighting the Germans who had overrun their country. Among the Whitley's crew was a Jugoslav officer who assisted in the recognition of the correct drop areas.

Initially the Jugoslav resistance had been led by a right wing Army Officer, General Michaelovic, but after an internal power struggle inside the country, the Allies came to appreciate that the Communist resistance fighters under their leader, Tito, were the patriots most likely to inflict damage upon the Germans. Thereafter, loads of valuables were dropped, by pre-arranged ground signals, to Tito's men.

The temptation of seeing such vast wealth being literally thrown overboard proved too much for some of the NCOs of Austin's crew. Accordingly, they hijacked the contents of one canister (the aircraft usually carried about a dozen), filling it with sand. Austin was a conscientious officer and it so happened that on the night in question, low level cloud obscured the drop zone. Despite the almost desperate pleas of the men involved in the deception to jettison the load, Austin decided to return with it to Luqa.

Even then they might have got away with it but the canisters were rechecked before being flown out again and the plot discovered. However, it was not obvious who was responsible for substituting sand for gold.

The first Austin knew of it was when he was advised that his room was to be searched. Innocent but puzzled, he agreed. As he expected nothing was found. Only then he was confronted with the news of the theft. As the captain of the aircraft he was a prime suspect although, if so, he would surely have made sure the canister went out over Jugoslavia, or even into the sea?

At one point it was even suggested he might like to go alone into his room with a loaded revolver and 'do the decent thing'!

Inevitably, after biding their time, some part of the loot began to appear in Valletta. It was easily traced back to the miscreants who were promptly arrested and jailed. As might be expected – it could only happen in Malta – this led to an almost bizarre event. One of the jailed NCOs was known to be an accomplished trumpet and saxophone player. Accordingly, when Christmas 1941 came around, he was let out of prison on Christmas Day on condition that, (a) he spent the morning at the dockyard helping to unload a ship, and (b) that he subsequently entertain the men by playing for them in the mess that evening!

There wasn't much to talk about in Malta so the whole affair became widely known. It is even reported that after the Whitley was destroyed on the ground – almost inevitable for any aircraft – a cushion seat was salvaged for use in the Ops Room. During a boisterous rag there some time later, the cushion was thrown at someone, missed, hit a wall and burst open to a showering of large denomination bank notes!

* * *

Whereas in Britain, the Wellington aircraft is almost solely known as a night bomber, its uses in the Middle East and Malta were much more varied. So much so that one Operational Signal once referred to – Goofingtons, Fishingtons, Flashingtons, Miningtons and even Bombingtons.

The Goofingtons were originally the name coined for the aircraft in which I and two other crews had. flown to Malta in September 1941. All three crews had come from 221 Squadron of Coastal Command and the aircraft were equipped with ASV (Air to Surface Vessel) Mark II, then a TOP SECRET airborne radar device. As can be seen in photos, the Wellingtons were festooned with additional aerials. They protruded under the nose, wings, atop the fuselage and along the fuselage sides. 221 Squadron had been using these Mark VIII Wellingtons for anti-U-boat operations over the Atlantic from a new airfield at Limavady, in Northern Ireland.

In Malta, I was soon put in charge of this Special Duties Flight where we found the ASV could pick up ships at 20 or 30 miles, sometimes at even greater distances. The Flight operated under the direct orders of Hugh Pughe Lloyd himself. On one occasion he used the initials ASV in a signal to me and was tactfully informed that this was prohibited due to the secret nature of the equipment. His next signal to me referred instead to 'my bloody instrument'. HP didn't relish correction!

For reasons that had no logic, a Wellington festooned with ASV aerials came to be known in Malta, and later elsewhere, as a 'Goofington', although sometimes they were referred to as 'Sticklebacks' for more obvious reasons. Various experiments were tried by my night flying crews in order to bring attacking forces to the ships which we discovered and were able to shadow at night. We only operated at night for during the day it was the Marylands of 69 Squadron which searched the seas for them.

At this stage of the war, only one person in Malta, a young Canadian, Pilot Officer Albert (Al) E Glazer, best understood the principles of radar. In consequence he was attached to the SDF, making a number of operational flights in our aircraft, although he was not officially aircrew. Much of the success of my SDF in Malta, was due to Glazer and to the three airmen radar technicians under him, LACs Few, Card and Rogers.

At this stage, the other two crews of the SDF were captained by Pilot Officer David Beaty, who later became a well known novelist, and Sergeant Dennis Reason. Our maintenance came under an ex-

Halton Brat, the tall, mustachioed, Flight Sergeant Dale.

Perhaps the unit's greatest success was achieved using the novel operational tactics which were worked out between myself and Captain W G Agnew RN, of *HMS Aurora*. This ship was the lead vessel of Naval Force K, which consisted of two light cruisers (*Aurora* and *Penelope*) and two small destroyers (*Lance* and *Lively*). Under Agnew's inspired leadership during the autumn and winter of 1941, they became the scourge of the enemy. They had come to Malta that autumn as soon as it was realised that the Luftwaffe had, for the time being, withdrawn most of its aircraft from Sicily, for the Russian front.

Air Vice Marshal Lloyd was quick to appreciate that my SDF and Agnew's ships, could work together for the benefit of both services. Neither of our units were allowed to venture out in broad daylight – there were still too many dive bombers (the Italians also used the Stuka which they called the Pichiatelli) and torpedo bombers as well as fighters. Force K was, however, permitted to depart about two hours before sunset, which gave it a 'window' of about 14 hours in which they could catch and sink any ships. Since they could cruise at up to 28 knots, their radius of action before daylight arrived extended to about 200 miles from the island. As Axis shipping usually kept at least 100 miles distance, it was only worth while despatching Force K after enemy ships had been accurately located and tracked.

How Agnew and I operated, briefly, was as follows. Thanks to Glazer's idea of installing a radar beacon (called a 'rooster') on the mast of *HMS Aurora*, the crews of the SDF were able to pick it up on the Wellington's ASV at a range of around 100 miles. Once we had located a ship or convoy, we could then direct Force K towards it. As a matter of interest, it was only years later that I appreciated what a gesture Captain Agnew RN made in agreeing to be directed into battle by an RAF acting Flight Lieutenant!

A novel code and signalling system was drawn up to use between Force K and the SDF aircraft. This gave Agnew all the information which he needed to know in order to be guided by the Goofington to the exact area where the aeroplane would be shadowing the target. Once within sight of the ship or convoy, with the aid of flares dropped from the aeroplane (when the moonlight glow was insufficient), Force K was able to sink the enemy from long range, before they knew what was happening.

Another means of getting attackers to ships found at night by the aircraft of the SDF, was developed with the Fleet Air Arm aeroplanes at Hal Far, as mentioned in an earlier chapter. Here again, it was Pilot Officer Glazer's technical ability which proved most useful.

In this instance he installed an ASV beacon inside the shadowing Wellington. This enabled the leader of the night formation of Swordfish or Albacores, to 'home' on to where the SDF aircraft was shadowing the enemy. This did depend entirely on 830 or 828 Squadron having one aircraft also equipped with ASV. When this was available the others would fly in formation with it. Thankfully a few of the FAA torpedo planes had been so equipped, even though their ASV was a crude Mark I; but good enough to home towards the SDF Wellington.

As always with all ASV operations, the apparatus of that period only worked with maximum effectiveness if the night air was relatively dry and if the sea conditions were fairly calm. As the winter weather of 1941 advanced – and it was particularly bad that year – ideal conditions became fewer and fewer. An additional drawback to effective operations was that none of the score or more of additional ASV aerials of my Goofingtons, were protected by any anti-ice or de-icing equipment. Consequently they soon became iced-up in the cold, damp air; reducing the already lowered performance of the aircraft as well as rendering the equipment almost useless.

* * *

The name of 'Fishington' was given to the Wellingtons which had been modified to carry either one, or two, Naval torpedoes. As already mentioned, the idea was first developed by 38 Bomber Squadron based near Cairo – Shallufa – and modified locally at the Maintenance Unit near there.

The torpedoes 'tin-fish' being Naval, were not designed to be dropped from the air but fired from ships or submarines. In order for the Wellington to accommodate them, the bomb-doors had to be chopped short. Experiments with the fitting of tail fins to the 'tin-fish', in order to prevent them breaking up on hitting the water, had to be carried out before a successful airborne technique of dropping them from Wellingtons could be developed. Eventually an effective method, which involved flying at about 60 feet with wings level, nose a degree or two up and at a speed of 140 knots, was determined. Then, and only then, would the torpedo run straight and true.

These early Fishingtons (some later developments were called 'Torpingtons' when equipped with both ASV and torpedoes) –

except for the one 'eclipse of the moon' operation mentioned earlier – did not operate from Malta but initially only in the Middle East. Later in the UK, in 1942, a stream of ASV equipped Fishington aircraft and crews, were arriving in the Middle East and Malta. Virtually all crews had been trained at No 7 (C) OTU at Limavady, then Abbotsinch near Glasgow, and later at the big Torpedo Training Unit at Turnberry. I know, because I had then become the officer in charge of the Torpedo Training Flight at all these places.

Some of the Fishingtons were incorporated into Luqa's resident 69 Squadron. In addition, 221 Squadron, the unit which had first used ASV Wellingtons over the Atlantic, converted to Torpingtons and for a while they too operated from Luqa. Later, an Australian Squadron, No 458, was also based at Luqa; principally with Fishingtons.

Although initially these Fishingtons/Torpingtons scored many important night successes – especially in the hands of such men as the Canadian, Flying Officer Harry W 'Hawk' Donkersley, whose sinking of vital tankers rapidly earned him the DFC and bar, they soon ran out of targets to attack. By then the battle of Alamein had already been won and the North African war was progressing well. Meantime, Wellingtons were used on anti-submarine work and for mining enemy ports – the latter known inevitably as 'Miningtons'! Another variation was the 'Flashington', a Wellington equipped with flares which it dropped to illuminate enemy ships and targets at night.

After having described all this, it may come as a surprise that the Wellingtons were also used for their originally intended purpose while on Malta – night bombing, hence 'Bombingtons'! (Presumably a name given in order to distinguish them for the myriad of others uses to which the old Wimpy was being put.) At periods during 1940–42, Wellington bombers of 37, 38, 104 and 148 Squadrons had all spent time at Luqa, in order to raid such targets as Tripoli, Naples, Palermo, and enemy airfields, etc. So close were the targets, that on some nights it was possible to fly two or even three operations, crews changing as the Wimpy was bombed-up again. Happily their losses over the targets were low, despite Italian flak displays, but losses on the ground to enemy raids and strafing attacks were calamitous. Luqa became a graveyard for scores of these aircraft.

Finally there was just one offbeat operation that well might have caused one particular Wellington aircraft to be dubbed a 'Boozington'. As might be expected, this involved the unpredictable Adrian Warburton. With all the wrecked Wellingtons strewn about, and with Christmas approaching, Warby spotted a

Wimpy which, while it had been damaged and 'written off,' didn't look in too bad a condition. Persuading his devoted airmen to try and patch it up, and with almost unlimited spares from other wrecks to hand, they eventually got it into a state which seemed flyable. Warby took a week's leave and got the Wimpy which officially didn't exist, off the ground and flew it to Egypt. Having meantime raised a sizeable sum of money, he bought up hundreds of bottles of booze, then flew back to the island.

A carefully arranged reception committee awaited his return and the plan was to have the booze taken away and hidden until Christmas. However, the secret had leaked out and a rival gang with another lorry met the Wellington and hijacked the whole valuable load! Although this was all totally unofficial, certain Military Police were in on the plot and they eventually tracked down the missing bottles – hidden above the ceiling of the padre's office! This padre was clearly one of enterprise. Later he was unfrocked for bigamy! UK was most certainly never like that.

It is not known how much of this story was brought to the attention of Hugh Pughe, and even if he did know about it, the chances are he would not have interfered. In his eyes Warby could do no wrong. However, one Group Captain definitely knew about the aircraft. Although this high ranking officer was only employed on ground duties on Malta, he used to fly it, with ground armourers as air gunners, on unofficial night bombing raids! (Presumably now a 'Nothington' since it did not officially exist?!) As was inevitable, the 'Boozington' was eventually bombed and destroyed on the ground; remaining this time, unrepairable.

* * *

After the publication of my autobiography 'In Full Flight' (in 1965)[1] I received a letter from a former Wireless Operator/Air Gunner who had been on 221 Squadron with me and later with SDF on Malta. A W Saunders had some splendid recollections of Wellingtons on Malta and I quote from his letter. He and his crew were on their way to the Middle East in 1942 but only got as far as Malta as by then I had learned the technique of hijacking aircraft en-route to the Middle East.

[1] Reissued 1991 by Wingham Press.

We landed at Malta perfectly, waited to be refuelled, when a flight lieutenant climbed in and told us to unload as we were staying. We protested violently and flatly refused to budge. Two more types climbed in and slightly more diplomatically pointed out that they did not want US but SDF wanted the aircraft! They assured us we would be sent on to join 221 by the first available aircraft. As I took part in this hijacking of Sticklebacks many times later, I noticed that the effect on the hijacked crew was invariably the same.

The next morning we had a serious crew talk and decided that, as individuals, we were efficient but when we operated collectively we had a jinx. We therefore decided that if we could, we would split up. This would have to wait until we could swap with others so, as we immediately started flying as Goofingtons for the Swordfish, we continued as a crew. It is ironical to think back now that we did four rapid trips during the following week, without trouble of any kind, and sank a small coaster into the bargain.

We eventually did split up at the end of the month when a few other SDF types were sent on rest to the ME and I joined Flight Lieutenant Le Masurier (Massey) as 1st Wireless Operator/Air Gunner. We carried on doing the trips with the Swordfish, interspersed with lone bombing trips, practically wholly confined to Rommel's supply line.

Force K were no more, in fact the only surface craft that could get in or out were the *Welshman* and the *Manxman* and these two brought in everything from matches to gun barrels. In June the rations were cut again – the livestock had already been killed off and we had eaten it, so that even the Black Market places closed down. Petrol was short and reserved for fighters and transit aircraft; so we were grounded for three weeks.

Then we got a few deliveries [of aviation fuel] by sub and started doing diversionary attacks for the Stringbags. Over Messina one night, we created a stink at one end of the town whilst the faithful FAA went in with torps. It was quite good fun, as with at the most, all three Wimpeys serviceable, our instructions were to 'make yourselves look a lot!' We worked out a pattern that by flying at different heights and coming in from different directions, we could give the impression of being a large force.

We then started to work with subs by modifying the Goofingtons to carry flares in the bomb bay, Warburton found the target and we went out at dusk to illuminate the subs as they came up. When working as illuminators we promptly became known as Flashingtons. This had only moderate success because of the difficulties of communication between sub and aircraft. (See Appendix) In August, just before the convoy, we were transferred to 69 Squadron as were the rest, so that we had three Goofingtons/Flashingtons, six Baltimores and Warby's Spitfire. Warby was made CO and up till then I had not met him although I had seen him from a distance. The very night we were merged – and unknown to me – Warby had decided to fly with us as front gunner to see how the other half lived. Arriving at dispersal just before midnight, I immediately climbed into the front turret to load the guns which was a hell of a job. That night we were flying with a substitute rear gunner, as Bob Fairhurst, our regular man was down with 'Malta Dog'.

Shortly afterwards I was in the W/T compartment when I heard someone in the front turret and assumed it to be the other gunner checking things over. Having completed my job I was about to climb from the aircraft to have a last cigarette, when a very plaintive voice from the front turret said, 'I say, I'm awfully sorry but I seem to have unloaded the guns.' I could not see in the dark of course and immediately thought it was the new chap, so I said, 'It serves you f— — — well right, now you'll have to load 'em again.' But he replied, 'But I can't; you'd better do it.' This made me absolutely livid. I jumped up to the back of the turret, grabbed the occupant by the back of his battle dress, yanked him out and swung myself in. He offered to help but I told him where to go and we continued in this happy fashion until I had finished. I then heaved myself out and as he was still standing on the bomb-aimer's mat, I landed heavily on his feet. This gave me some satisfaction, particularly as I heard him gasp. I then prodded him before me, saying, 'And now, get out, you're neither use nor ornament, I want a smoke.' As he climbed down the ladder and came under the downward indent. light, I saw he had three thick bars on his shoulders. It was, of course, Warby! As I was still only a flight sergeant, visions of Court

Martial swam across my mind. Anyway, he offered me a cigarette and asked if I would give him some dual on the guns one day. He was as good as his word and was a very apt pupil. He subsequently flew with us several times and we became good friends.[2]

Later on seven or eight Torpedo Wimpeys arrived, from 98 Squadron, I think. These promptly became known as Fishingtons and were taken into the 'family' under the 69 banner. With these, we worked out a system similar to those used when working with the subs. Warby, in daylight found the targets, and we took off at dusk to their estimated position. When we found the ships we shadowed them, called up the Fishingtons and then strapped our W/T key down for, I think, two minutes in every three, whilst the Fishingtons homed on us by loop. When they got near they called us up individually by a simple code, for illumination. We then dropped sticks of flares for each one as he did his run in. From the Wireless Operator's point of view it was ideal, because he was busy all the time instead of the usual period of boredom, but, of course, as soon as you start strapping your key down in the middle of enemy territory, you stick your neck out. Surprisingly enough, only twice did we appear to attract night fighters. Either Jerry was not quite with it or we were off before they could find us. We had evidence that Jerry was experimenting with radar for his night fighters in that one homed on us one night and followed us for over an hour without firing. We did all sorts of things to try and get rid of him. Massey almost stood the Wimpy on its tail but he still followed, until he turned off a few miles from Malta. Apart from giving us the fright of our lives – particularly Bob Fairhurst in the rear turret, who's eyes were like organ stops when we landed – he gained nothing but experience.

Although little has been written about them, it is known that Malta harboured at different times, at least two enemy built float planes which were used for top secret operations. One was a twin engined Heinkel 115 which had been with Norwegian Coastal Air Forces pre-war. When Norway fell in April 1940, at least two of these German aircraft had been flown to England and one at least ended

---

[2] Although the author can find 359 Malta operations in Warburton's log books, he never entered any unofficial ones in Wellingtons, Liberators. Many have now come to light.

up in Malta. It was kept under wraps at Kalafrana and only ventured from its hiding place at night, probably flown solely by a crew of the Norwegian Air Force. It had been modified to carry a person inside of one of the floats!

Eventually the large seaplane hangars at Kalafrana were bombed to destruction during the winter of 1941, but it is understood that before then the He115 had departed on one dark night and had failed to return from one of its clandestine missions.

The other enemy built floatplane was the Cant Z506 which Lieutenant Strever and his crew had hijacked while prisoners of war (see Chapter 8). There is no evidence that this was ever used by the Allies but equally, there seems no good reason why such a captured prize should not have featured in some sort of escapade. It was eventually flown to England.[3]

During the spring of 1943, an Air Sea Rescue Swordfish pilot, Sergeant Cohen, was on a long-range search when the aircraft experienced engine trouble. Unable to get back to Malta, he managed to crash-land safely on the small Italian island of Lampedusa. Visions of capture and of ending his days in a POW camp, floated before him. However, the islanders had had enough of Mussolini and the Germans, and as by then, Tripoli and Tunis had fallen, they could see that the war in that part of the Mediterranean was lost.

The leading citizens and the island militia, far from taking Sergeant Cohen prisoner, decided to surrender to him and accordingly, they formally handed over the entire island to him! Lampedusa stayed in Allied hands thereafter, while Sergeant Cohen became known among his colleagues, as the 'King of Lampedusa'!

---

[3] One report indicates that it was used on at least one air-sea rescue search for a Beaufort crew which had ditched.

CHAPTER FOURTEEN

EXTRACTS FROM A DIARY

Leading Aircraftman Bill Metcalf kept a diary while on Malta, and what follows covers the period March to July 1942 during the very worst period of the bombing. The authentic diary is, naturally, very much longer, but these extracts of his splendid writings tell the story of the terrible siege and blitz; far better than any post-war researcher could do.

Two unusual factors helped to keep Bill sane and rational despite the hell that was going on all around him. One was that he befriended a stray mongrel dog which he called Cherry, the other that, being something of a jazz musician, he could take himself off to play at a dance or simply to join in with others, in an 'ad hoc' jam session. In this way he was able to relax and lose himself in the music.

During the period covered, Bill, like so many others, was struck down with the dreaded Malta Dog and influenza, yet he never reported sick. He, like so many others with that true sense of responsibility, knew he had to carry on – and he did.

Although Bill Metcalf's tally of enemy aircraft seen destroyed does not stand up to post-war analysis, he is correct in that he is accurately recording what he and others believed true at the time. Battle claims and losses have always been difficult to substantiate, but in the heat of battle, who can say truthfully what has actually occurred.

1942. March 6: Worst raid of the war last night, my head is splitting with the effects of concussion and blast. At one time I thought old Cherry was going mad. The Hurricanes got another seven kites down and they've been in action again today. At noon we were brought back to Ta Kali and set on making roads from the dispersal points with picks and shovels; it's nearly broken my back. A Me 109 has just been shot down on the aerodrome.

March 7: Spitfires have arrived at last! Sixteen of them escorted by Blenheims. Also arrived, five Beaufighters for the MNFU. After another hectic night, but the mere sight of the new arrivals brought the morale up 50% of every bloke on the station. We started straight away taking the Spits' overload tanks off and hope to get at least four or five ready by noon tomorrow. (Compare this with the 9–15 minutes of 9 May!)

March 8: Managed to get six Spitfires ready for action and what a job it's been. I haven't worked so hard since I joined the RAF. Luqa got several more bashings but we were left alone to work!

March 9: Not much happened last night except the Beaus shot down a Ju 88. Squadron Leader Westmacott also shot down an 88 and probable He 111. Eight Spitfires start operations tomorrow and I hope they come up to expectations.

March 12: Feel absolutely washed out this morning. Beau shot down a Heinkel. At noon we got news of a big [radar] plot so Cherry and I 'dispersed' over the fields and only just in time, because a shower of 88s bombed Ta Kali; Chalky White and Heckmondwike were killed with five more trapped (in the rubble).

March 14: My Spit 'B' got another victim and now has three swastikas on its fuselage.

March 15: The usual raids today. During one, a Me 109 dived to machine-gun and, without looking, I jumped straight over a wall and landed up to my chest in goat manure! Our Spits are now belting old Jerry and the Hurricanes and the ack-ack are still battling!

March 17: Seven raids during the night. 88s bombed the camp at noon and a bus load of labourers stopped a packet. All kites in action again and I saw one Spitfire hit the drink but we should have a good score between us.

March 18: Six night raids. Hal Far caught a packet this morning, Luqa at noon and Ta Kali all afternoon! One Spitfire shot down, also five Hurricanes. Hurricane and a Beaufighter burnt out and a 800 gallon petrol bowser still burning, plus two more Spits u/s. Several times I thought Cherry and I had 'had it' and then some guy says Jerry has left Sicily. He has – for Malta!

March 19: Bowser burning till after midnight. First day off for weeks so I took Cherry down to St Anton's gardens. Walking back for tea we had to duck into a sort of semi-surface shelter down Attard Road as four Ju 88s dived onto

Ta Kali. A Spitfire and another of the Beaus burnt out.

March 20: Pay Day. It is now 9.05 pm and I've just come through the worst blitz that's ever been known in England, Germany or Malta, and all of it on Ta Kali. It is estimated that at least 250 kites of various makes took part and the 800 odd bombs that were dropped were made up of all shapes and sizes. Huddled in that slit trench with poor little Cherry and four other chaps, I thought the end had come. Billets were blown up right and left. Two more petrol bowsers on fire; Spitfires, Hurricanes, Beaus, Blenheims and the odd Maryland, all lying wrecked and smouldering. The smell of cordite and the crash of falling bombs added to the hellish row of the ack-ack barrage and has sent me more or less stone deaf. My billet has come through OK – minus windows and a bit of roof.

March 21: Lofty Bond was killed two minutes after I left him last night. The Ta Kali blitz continued again this morning by approximately 200 bombers. The ack-ack shot down fourteen Ju 88s and the only four serviceable Hurricanes shot down four Me 109s. Imtarfa hospital was hit and just on noon our Officer's mess at Point de Vue was hit and six killed. Other casualties not yet known but 40 known to be dead in a shelter, hit at Mosta. When things calmed down, Corporal Harker and I had one look over the drome and set off to get drunk. There didn't look to be a single square yard without a bomb crater! Anyhow, after walking to Imtarfa, Rabat and then Mosta, we gave it up and set off to our billet. Halfway we had another raid and I had to lie face down in a wet field to miss the flying rocks from the bombs.

March 22: Haven't had the strength to move all day so I just lie in bed and hoped and hoped… Twice the remains of the camp were machine-gunned but I was below the window level. Haven't had a wash for three days and feel absolutely filthy and as hungry and thirsty as Hell. There is no water or anything on the whole camp.

March 23: This isn't a life, it's just existence! Hurricanes shot down two more 88s yesterday. I was so hungry this morning, not having eaten, or washed, for three days, I raided the grub store and found a tin of bully beef, a tin of plums and a tin of hard biscuits. After that feast I walked over to Luqa to help with the Spits. Another daylong air raid during which a small convoy got into harbour. Weather very bad for fighters but we shot down five and the Navy boys got another five. *HMS Renown* is in Grand Harbour,[1] damaged, and the old *Breconshire* had to be beached at Kalafrana with the remains of an 88 on her deck. Still only myself and four chaps from 69 Squadron living on camp!

March 24: Raid free night for a change. Early today two Spits shot down two Jerry recce planes. Luftwaffe over in full force at 10 am and his Ju 88s and Stukas gave Grand Harbour the same as we've had for the past fortnight at Ta Kali. In the third raid they were 'jumped' by our fighters and let their bomb load go on Hal Far. 'B' Dugout and the NAAFI shelter got direct hits and the number of chaps killed is thought to be very high.

March 27: Dozens of alerts today but very few bandits crossed the coast. 229 Squadron – Hurricanes – arrived from Middle East. We worked all night getting the overload tanks off, ready for Hal Far tomorrow. The bomb blasts have definitely upset Cherry; she's been sick all day and is going very thin.

April 3: And a Good Friday it's been too! Grand Harbour, Luqa, Hal Far and Ta Kali each dive-bombed several times by Stukas and Ju 88s. I had a couple more near squeaks, but then, who didn't? No flying due to u/s kites and now there are more of them u/s. Should have drawn my pay today but I was much too busy for a little thing like that!

April 6: This Easter has been one that I'll remember (should I be one of the lucky ones who get away with it). From dawn to dusk, wave after wave of 88s, 87s and other gash kites have bombed and bombed. During one lull I bobbed my head above the slit trench and suddenly spotted a fresh wave of 88s coming in over St Pauls. I counted twenty-seven but when the leader put his nose down and started a power-dive straight for me – what a sensation; I could neither speak nor move! Luckily it came a few feet too low and the bombs went over the top of the trench.

---

[1] I do not think *HMS Renown* was in Malta - author.

April 7: And still they come in all their might. Heaven alone knows what's going to happen next and where this is all going to end. It's a pity we haven't some fighter protection, but what we do have has done wonderful work and each pilot deserves a Victoria Cross at least. To send the last few up alone would be murder in the first degree. The ack-ack boys too are great and I hold my hand out to each of them.

April 11: Reuters from London says the raids here have now equalled anything London has ever had even in the Battle of Britain. The ack-ack has just about run out of ammo so the barrage has been nil. Twice during the day I thought Cherry and I were booked for the long journey. Both bombs were delayed action and all I got was a smack on the shoulder by a lump of rock.

April 12: Being Sunday I expected tricks and we got them. For an hour Messerschmitts came over Ta Kali shooting up everything in sight – and everybody. One came over the ditch we were lying in and his cannon shells were whizzing over the top like hailstones.

April 17: Only drew £3 for pay instead of the £6 I was expecting. The King awarded the George Cross to the people and garrison of Malta. I can't see what good that will do – a bit of decent grub for a change and some cigarettes would have been more appreciated by the men.

April 20: The new Spitfires arrived at 11.45 and were in action by 2 o'clock. Fifty came – seven down so far.

April 21: All raids today are on Ta Kali. No idea he had so many bombers, it's just one endless stream. Fired away with rifles, Tommy guns and twin Vickers K guns but the bullets just bounce off. We claim damage on two Ju 88s and a Me 109 from the armoury roof.

April 22: I've been on the armoury roof and once on the CO's K[2] guns, I put a burst into the starboard engine of an 88 and set it on fire – I wonder if it came down? Now I've come through OK it seems great fun but I suppose I'll be stretching my luck too far once too often and then…

[2] Wing Commander Jack Satchell had set up his own private gun post. It claimed several victories.

April 23: I got dragged out of bed at 4.35 am to fix up a kite. It was so urgent that I worked through two raids to finish it. It took me till 10.45. I was walking away with my tool kit as the next warning sounded so I did a crafty nip into the slit trench about 25 yards away. Next time I looked, there was bugger-all of the Spitfire left! Was I annoyed! Of the 50 that came in on Monday we have twelve left.

April 27: Last night we lost Flight Sergeant Wood from Huddersfield in the MNFU Hurricane somewhere over Sicily. Biggest raids today have been proper Itie style with bigger and better bombs. The crater of one was large enough to have floated the Queen Mary. Ammo truck full of hand grenades got a direct hit. Only three serviceable Spitfires left now and, as Jerry seems to be going all out for gun positions, etc, I'm wondering if after all, he's going to try and invade the island?

April 28: I'm cheesed off to the limit. It's just a year since I landed here and what a change has taken place in it since then. Can't help wishing we had stayed in the Middle East.

April 30: The CO of Ta Kali, Wing Commander Satchell, is posted. Wing Commander Gracie is now in charge. We had a full parade at 10.30 am, complete with webbing and rifles, just to tell us he was boss. If only half his promises come true things will be OK. This morning Me 109s had the Spits running in circles for half an hour, strafing each one that tried to land. The erks got one down with rifle fire and the Spits got one Me and two Ju 88s.

May 2: Cigarette issue now cut to ten a week and the bread ration down to three-quarters of rotolo (Maltese measure, about 10 oz) – next thing we'll be turning out to grass!

May 6: Don't know whether we had any night raid or not. I was so tired that after putting a request for early call at 03.45, I went to bed and fell asleep straight away. We're expecting 100 Spitfires this week and after them, a big convoy. If the latter gets spitchered (a commonly used English version of a Maltese word meaning finished/destroyed), well I guess Malta would have 'had it'.

May 7: Big preparations going on for this lot of Spitfires and what the CO calls the Battle of Malta. We're expecting bags of action and casualties, and I find myself stuck on No 26 pen – the worst of the lot – it's by the old HQ.

May 8: Full parade on eastern dispersal for final detail of our plan for tomorrow. We spent all day getting fuel, oil, ammo, glycol, etc, to each aircraft pen, although we were strafed and bombed. Our beds having been taken for incoming officers, Ken and I slept on the deck!

May 9: Zero Hour! Fifty Spitfires arrived in the middle of a raid. Talk about organisation – ten minutes after the Spits arrived, they were airborne and going into action. Four raids, including two by the 'big five' (five Italian bombers that came over daily in close formation and ignored everything) and a large part of their 'presents' were left at Ta Kali. My pen must have been their target judging by how many near misses it got. One of the chaps had only landed at 4.00 pm, in a Catalina, straight from England. He'd never seen a bomb let alone been so close to one and I couldn't help feeling sorry for him. Total score today is seven down, seven Probables and fifteen Damaged. We lost three Spits and four crash-landed. Only a few casualties.

May 10: The best day's work I've seen in the RAF. Started work at 2.00 pm and finished at 9.15 pm. Talk about dogfights; for one raid we had 21 Spits from Ta Kali, 16 from Luqa and nine and six Hurricanes from Hal Far. Between them we got 26 confirmed and a whole lot of Probables. We lost two!

May 14: Jerry is getting fed up with Ta Kali Spitfires and he's been trying to liquidate them all day. One Ju 88 was shot down just off the perimeter of the aerodrome and all the crew were left in it to roast.

May 15: Mostly fighter sweeps today and have our boys made whoppee! Lord Douglas-Hamilton, the CO of 603 Squadron, shot down a Macchi 202 and a Me 109 while flying my machine. Fed up with working 16 and 17 hours a day.

May 16: At noon Corporal French, a new lad from Blighty, and a soldier, were killed by the 'big five' (Italian bombers). It shook me rotten. On duty from 05.00 to 17.30, then on standby till 06.00.

May 17: Chief Stanwictz has taken Frenchie's death pretty bad and he chewed me up horribly for doing a re-arm during an air raid! Before, he used to go mad if we took cover.

May 30: Went to Valletta, first time since Christmas, just to get big eats. I had four dinners at different places at a total cost of 14/9d [74 pence].

May 31: Worked from 3.00 am to 9.30 pm on half a sausage, a slice of bread and a mug of tea without sugar; then our MO wants to know how it is that 90% of the camp is feeling poorly. I'm full of cold and have a dose of the Malta Dog.

June 5: Very bad day. First thing on dawn patrol, I didn't fasten a panel securely enough and the wind blew it off while taxiing for take-off. Got a good chewing up. Later a kite needed rearming just because a stupid pilot had a burst at a seagull! I was so cheesed off that I wasn't paying attention and let off a burst of twenty rounds – straight over the crew room. I was darned lucky to miss a Court-Martial!

June 8: Started work at 03.00 on a breakfast of one slice of bread, one spoonful of mashed potato and a mug of tea without sugar. Our next bite was 14.35 pm – exactly 11½ hours later. No wonder half the chaps are on their knees.

June 15: From 08.00 to 18.00 we've kept up an eight-plane patrol and a twenty-plane escort to the Beauforts. The convoy has been getting bashed all day but it was out of our reach. My kite has just come back from patrol and the pilot says all he can see of the seven merchantmen is two, and a tanker towed by a destroyer a long way behind.

June 25: 249 Squadron shot down two and got a Spit very badly shot up. Flight Sergeant M E Tomkins was the pilot; he tried very hard to bring his kite in with a very bad glycol leak. As soon as he lowered his flaps he nose-dived into the deck and burst into flames. We'd no chance to get him out at all. I swore blind after the Blenheim fire, for which Sergeant Louttit got the BEM,[3] that I'd never go near another fire as long as I was in the RAF but as usual, I was

---

[3] This occurred on 19 January, 1942, when a Blenheim had been set on fire during a raid. Corporal D Louttit helped to put out flames on two bowsers and then ran to the aircraft to stuff rags into holes in the Blenheim's fuel tanks. He then drained the tanks to save the fuel and later helped put out flames. LACs Bill Metcalf and Curly Revell managed to take out the ammunition and radio from the aircraft before the fire tender arrived.

on the job as all the others were down the hole and I was in the slit trench. When the fire engine did come I grabbed a hose and jumped on the main plane – the rest of the blokes seemed scared of the flying cannon shells and were busy arguing whether or not it was a waste of time bothering. I was soaked to the skin in chemical foam and full of blisters and burns. Pilot's remains smelt something awful and the sight made me sick as a dog.

June 30: Sergeant Valentine, flying my new X-K, replacement for X-O, shot down but he got a bomber and a fighter first and as he was going down he took a Me 109 with him for luck. DFM? X-O is the third kite of mine to go into the drink in three days. Each kite was out of No 2 pen and each pilot has baled out OK.

July 5: This morning I think I had one of my closest shaves yet. Leo, Jock and I were in the slit trench behind our pen when a container of anti-personnel bombs dropped less than five yards away. It nearly buried and choked us as well as poor old Cherry.

July 6: Another near miss by anti-personnel bombs in the 07.00 raid. The kite in my pen was a write-off. That's two days in succession!

July 8: In today's first raid Pilot Officer King and Flight Lieutenant Saunders were shot down. King failed to bale out. I nearly cried when I heard because he's the greatest guy I've ever met and that's saying a lot. Lord Gort VC gave us a congratulatory message for our smashing week against the Nazis. Today we added another nine to our score and also got another load of bombs on Ta Kali.

By this date in Bill's diary, the tide of battle had turned. Malta was winning. The major problem had become how to get enough to eat. Unless a convoy with food on board could reach Malta, the air victories would have been won in vain.

Operation Pedestal in August 1942, with the arrival of the *Ohio* and the four merchantmen, provided the breather necessary to keep the patient alive. The arrival in November of all the ships of the convoy, Operation Stoneage, finally broke the siege. Against all the odds Malta had survived and by 1943 had become the springboard for the reclamation of Europe from the south.

No praise can be too high for the suppliers and defenders who had made all this possible. It was my privilege to have been kept alive and operational by such men and women. It is something that I can never forget.

EPILOGUE

Was Malta worth all the effort? Was it worth all the suffering? To answer these questions it is necessary to go back to the months of September, October and November 1941.

This was the period after the Luftwaffe had withdrawn virtually all its aircraft and aircrew from Sicily. They had left earlier in the year in order to become a part of Hitler's great offensive against Russia. By September 1941, the Allies had re-stocked Malta with warships and strike aircraft. They had been brought to the island for the purpose of attacking the supply ships which carried all the paraphernalia of war to the Italian and German (Axis) forces in the North African desert, by then already under the command of the brilliant German general, Erwin Rommel – the famed 'Desert Fox'.

These supply ships departed from ports in Sicily and Southern Italy and headed for those of the Axis forces. The only well-equipped harbour in North Africa was Tripoli; with Benghazi as a secondary port as dock facilities there were very sparse.

A glance at a map of the central Mediterranean shows that these Axis supply ships had to pass by Malta, strategically located to be a continual thorn in Rommel's side – if allowed to be so. Already these Axis ships, often in small but well protected convoys, were being hounded and attacked by the torpedo carrying Swordfish of 830 Squadron, FAA, but only at night, due to the fact that, with only an attack speed of 90 knots, it would have been suicide in daylight. The enemy was also being attacked, both during daylight and night hours, by the small but efficient submarines of the Royal Navy's 10th Flotilla at Lazaretto Creek, Sliema. However, most supplies got through and Rommel with his Afrika Korps leading the way, was receiving sufficient fuel and ammunition so as to pose a serious threat to the British 8th Army protecting Egypt, the Suez Canal and the Arabian oilfields beyond.

However, once the Allied Chiefs of Staff realised that the Luftwaffe had departed Sicily and that the bombing of Italy's Regia Aeronautica, once again on its own against Malta, was largely ineffective, the situation changed dramatically.

The Admiralty sent Force K to the island and the RAF flew in Blenheim and Wellington squadrons. The RAF also introduced into the struggle the Special Duties Flight with ASV radar equipped Wellingtons. Warburton and the other able 69 Squadron pilots and aircrew, in their Marylands, had for a year or more been successful in finding the enemy ships by day, now the SDF aircraft were to locate and shadow them by night.

Both day and night reconnaissance operations were much aided by the wealth of intelligence reports about the enemy's shipping movements which always seemed to be available in Malta. At that time, I, and no doubt all others except for Malta's supreme commanders, attributed such prior information about the enemy's intentions – including such details as actual sailing dates, times, etc, to Naval Intelligence backed up by 69 Squadron's almost daily photo-reconnaissance sorties of their ports.

However, it is now known that the Ultra intercepts, as deciphered by the 'boffins' at Bletchley Park, in England, probably provided an even more significant insight into the enemy's movements. Nevertheless, to guard against the enemy becoming suspicious of our finding their ships, it was always necessary to 'find' them more ostentatiously with reconnaissance aircraft, and not just go for an attack, even though the 'brass' knew, on most occasions, more or less where they might be found.

The success achieved against enemy shipping during those months of September to November 1941, speak for themselves:

September	38.5% tonnage sunk by Allies
October	63.0% tonnage sunk by Allies
November-	77.0% tonnage sunk by Allies

No side could possibly withstand such damaging losses and it is no surprise that, after November, the enemy ceased even to try to run merchant ships to Tripoli past Malta. The few that tried to run the gauntlet took the longer semi-circle eastward passage to Benghazi. Field Marshal Rommel and his forces found themselves being starved of virtually everything needed to continue the war in the desert. Something had to be done – and was done!

Luftlotte II, an entire Luftwaffe air army, was swiftly transferred from the Russian front to airfields in Sicily. This was one of three air armies facing the massive Russian front. By this date, the successful

German armies were sweeping all before them, even approaching the outskirts of Moscow itself. Another German army had surrounded and isolated mighty Leningrad, with the result that this great Russian city was steadily being starved to death. Although the first chill of the Russian winter was upon them, victory seemed assured. They could well have used the extra air support that was now taken from them. It is significant that after Luftlotte II departed, Hitler's armies got no further than the outskirts of Moscow!

It can, therefore, be argued that Malta's plight and the terrible 'blitz' of that 1941–42 winter, was Moscow's saviour; even that the transfer of Luftlotte II was a turning point of the war in Europe. Moreover, having once started to bomb and strafe Malta to such an extent that it became impossible for either the Royal Navy or Royal Air Force to attack the Axis flow of supplies to North Africa, Hitler found himself obliged to continue to keep on doing so. It was a case of abandoning Rommel, either that, or giving the order for the planned invasion of Malta.

The success of an invasion – often rumoured among the island's defenders – for which 100,000 troops had been assembled and were standing by, depended on support from the Italian Navy. Quite apart from the oil and arms which would have to be consumed, Hitler was reluctant to trust German troops, and elite paratroops in particular, to the care of the Italians. Goring was against an invasion too, as he, as well as Hitler, had been shaken by the number of casualties incurred, of both paratroops and transport crews and aircraft, during the capture of Crete in May 1941. All the while, of course, these 100,000 troops were sitting on their hands in France, while they might have been usefully employed in either North Africa or even Russia.

There was now a curious cat and mouse game between respective Allied and Axis High Commands. For as long as Luftlotte II continued to reduce Malta, its harbours and airfields, to rubble, then supplies could reach Rommel with some degree of surety. But almost within a week or two of withdrawing this air command and allowing the island a respite from its incessant pounding, the Allies would bring back the surface ships, submarines and strike aircraft in order once again to cut into the German supply line across the Mediterranean.

It was also to the German's disadvantage that, by having to base over 600 aircraft in Sicily, the Luftwaffe was, in effect, now fighting the Allied air forces on four widely spaced fronts. The Luftwaffe already had to keep a sizeable defensive force in Germany, the Low Countries and France, to oppose the ever increasing RAF and now USAAC bombing raids over Western Europe. It already needed to keep an air force in the desert in order to support Rommel, and of course, the Eastern Front of Russia, was daily eating up the German's air power in that vast arena.

Whether it was on the Home Front, in Russia or Tripolitania, Luftlotte II was much needed elsewhere, rather than be based on Sicily in order to mercilessly pound Malta into submission – a state never seriously contemplated either by the islanders or the defenders. Of the total German bomber force in the Mediterranean, over one half was in Sicily; also one third of their fighter force. They were all there solely to neutralise Malta. Malta suffered but its agonies were not in vain. The Luftwaffe in the Desert were outnumbered and ultimately decimated.

* * *

Another important aspect was that by 1942, the war in Europe, Russia and the Mediterranean had become less of a war of rapid movement and more a war of attrition. Sooner or later, the Axis forces, unless victorious in capturing the oil fields of Arabia and also those of southern Russia (Caucasus region), would start to run short of fuel – the lifeblood of modern warfare – as well as other natural resources that Germany and Italy lacked. The German war machine needed iron ore and copper, two of the metals the Allies possessed in almost infinite quantities. Once Rommel had been stopped short of Cairo, the lack of crude oil became even more critical to the Germans.

From November 1941 onwards, the heroic defenders and suppliers of Malta, did they but know it, were steadily helping to drain away this very lifeblood of their enemy's war machine.

Luftlotte II was not just a large air army; it was also a very experienced, efficient and deadly one. Its pilots and crews were, on the whole, veterans who were more battle hardened than those flying the Hurricanes and early Spitfires opposed to it. These brave and skilful men of Luftlotte II would have been of priceless worth both to the German troops battling their way through to Moscow as well as to the Afrika Korps facing superior RAF and SAAF numbers in the desert campaign. Luftlotte II might also have helped save the German cities and factories of the Homeland, being hit both day and night by the British and American heavy bombers.

History now tells us that both Moscow and Leningrad survived; that the German armies never quite reached the Russian oil fields; that Rommel's dream of advancing into Arabia evaporated at Alamein and that, thanks to the Battle of the Atlantic being turned in the Allies' favour, the might of American production would reach Britain and so ensure that the Allies would achieve final victory in the battle of attrition.

So 'Yes' it was worth it. Malta did certainly play a vital part in the overall plans for victory. It helped defeat the Afrika Korps, kept a large air army occupied and helped to end Mussolini's dream of conquest in the Mediterranean.

In saying this, it has to be said that the earlier, general, view when contemplating the desert war, was that so long as the British armies in North Africa could hold out against the German and Italian forces, Malta could just be held. It was only after the winter of 1941, when Axis bombing almost rendered Malta impotent, that a more realistic view was taken. This was the reverse; it was only then fully realised that only if Malta held out and was used as an offensive base – an unsinkable aircraft carrier – from which to harry Axis supply routes, could the troops in the desert be sure of not only holding out against Rommel, but eventually winning against him. It was then that all out efforts were made to ensure that the island did not give in. First it was supplied with Spitfires, then, at tremendous cost in ships and men, the island was supplied with just enough food, fuel and ammunition to enable it to stay in business.

Both the German and Italian post-war records show that, what they called the Battle for Cyrenaica, was lost months before the actual fighting on land sealed Rommel's fate. It was the failure of the Axis to provide Rommel with the fuel and other urgent supplies that he needed that made his defeat by the much larger opposing armies, backed by their dominating Air Forces, inevitable. Both German and Italian records make much of the role that the strikes by the RN and RAF from Malta played in denying Rommel the essentials he needed to reach Alexandria and Cairo.

So without doubt, Malta's defiance and resistance was most definitely worth while. All praise must therefore be given to the island's gallant defenders and suppliers. If they had wavered and cracked under the stupendous pressure to which the men were subjected, the island would have been lost and much else in WWII would have been very, very different. Any subsequent invasion of Sicily and Italy, for instance, would have needed an allied retake of Malta had it fallen. The loss of the Suez Canal and the Arabian oil fields may well have cost Britain the war; certainly the war in North Africa would have been lost.

It must never be forgotten that, without the support of the long suffering Maltese people who had to endure so much in a war that was not of their making, the RAF, and the other Services, could never have held out and ultimately have triumphed.

In the chaotic conditions created by the bombing, the opportunities for sabotage were unlimited.

In every way, from the great feats of Malta's own ack-ack gunners – the Royal Malta Artillery who lost the lives of 67 locals, to the humble washing of airmen's socks and shirts in the villages around the airfields, the Maltese peoples acted as if Britain's war was their war.

In the words that King George VI wrote in his own hand on 15 April 1942:

> To honour her brave people I award the George Cross to the island fortress of Malta to bear witness to a heroism and devotion that will long be famous in history.

None who underwent that baptism of fire can ever forget the experience. None who were there for any length of time emerged unchanged in one way or another. It broke a few. It made others. The most common regret among those who were there when the heat was on, is that they still have no personal emblem to show what they had to endure.[1] Only their memories remain, and the knowledge that they withstood the onslaught and came through victorious. Perhaps, after all, that is enough!

---

[1] The Malta Government in April 1992 rectified this omission by issuing a commemorative Malta Medal to both those who supplied and those who defended the islands 1940–1943.

FINALE

It is perhaps, fitting, to let the Royal Navy have the last words of this book. The Island of Malta and the British Navy have, after all, enjoyed over 100 years of friendly relations.

The following words are from a letter from Vice Admiral Sir Wilbraham Ford, Malta's Naval Commander, to Admiral of the Fleet, Viscount Andrew Cunningham of Hydhope, dated 3rd January 1942

I've given up counting the number of air raids we are getting. At the time of writing, 1600 hours, we have had exactly seven raids since 0900, quite apart from over a month of all night efforts. The enemy is trying to neutralise Malta's efforts, and, I hate to say, is gradually doing so. They've bust a sad number of our bombers and fighters, etc, and must continue to do so... Now we have Libya, and soon I trust, Tripoli, I consider Malta must be made stiff with MODERN fighters-Mosquitoes which can fly out from the UK on their own and Spitfires from Takoradi if a carrier cannot buzz them off. Guns and stores must come in by submarine beforehand. Just a bit of co-operation between Air and Admiralty and quite simple... The powers at home must give up safety first and send us out the latest if they want to hold Malta and use it as a base.

Minesweeping is now difficult and they appear to be laying them everywhere. Poor Abingdon, the only sweeper, and in daylight she got machine-gunned, eight casualties in Abingdon alone. I am trying to sweep during the dark hours... Work in the yard is naturally slowed up at present as a result of the raids... Until we get net defence I shall continue to be worried, especially for Marsamuscetto (harbour) and the submarines. Nothing really to stop them.

Why, Oh, why did they not press for my scheme of underground shelters! They would have been finished by now. As I write another bombing raid is just over and at least two more of ours burnt out.... Damnable to be quite useless.

Something must be done at once. How can I unload convoys I cannot think.

The date of this letter is very significant. Although the gallant Admiral, a tough, hard living, hard swearing man, cast in the traditional mould of a top British sea-dog, is almost despairing of Malta's survival, the real bombing hadn't even begun! The tonnage dropped in January 1942 was considerably less than one thousand. It reached 990 tons in February, rose to 2,170 tons in March, reaching 6,728 tons in April! By then, far from being 'Now we have Libya and soon I trust, Tripoli,' the British Army had been driven completely out of Libya and was in full retreat. Even Tobruk had fallen to the enemy.

YET MALTA STILL HELD

APPENDIX

Report by Acting Flight Lieutenant A Spooner, DFC on the operation of ASV Wellington operating from Malta, 1 October to 23 December 1941.This report was submitted direct to the AOC – Malta.

A flight of three long-range ASV Wellington aircraft, fitted with an auxiliary IFF set tuned so as to act as an ASV homing beacon, have been operating from Malta since 1 October 1941.

This flight is known as the Special Duties and is at present commanded by Acting Flight Lieutenant Spooner. The personnel consists of three aircrews captained by Acting Flight Lieutenant Spooner, Pilot Officer Beaty and Sergeant Reason and a technical section for the maintenance of the special equipment under the command of Flying Officer Glazer.

Attached hereto are the reports from Flying Officer Glazer, Pilot Officer Beaty and Sergeant Reason… (These have not survived, or not been found, in the Public Records Office.)

The flight operates only by night due to the proximity of Malta to enemy territory.

The flying personnel have all had considerable operational experience on long-range ASV aircraft prior to the forming of this flight, as they were drawn from No 221 GR Squadron which has been operating this type of A/C over the Atlantic since March 1941. The aircraft of 221 Squadron were not fitted with IFF set tuned to act as a homing ASV beacon.

This IFF homing beacon is referred to by the code word, 'Rooster'.

The Special Duties Flight has been used for the following work with a degree of priority corresponding with the order given hereunder:

1. Co-operating with Naval Forces based at Malta.

2. Co-operating with Swordfish aircraft at 830 Squadron.

3. Co-operating with Albacore aircraft of 828 Squadron.

4. Co-operating with Wellington aircraft of No 38, 104 and 40 Squadrons.

5. For night bombing attacks on enemy shipping.

6. For night shadowing of enemy shipping.

7. For sweeps along the enemy's known shipping lanes.

8. In addition there is the possibility that the aircraft may be employed against enemy submarines should they constitute a menace in the area.

9. There is also a scheme proposed whereby the aircraft should co-operate with our own submarines.

Taking each of these separately in turn the following is a summary of the experience gained.

1. Co-operation with Naval Forces

Before going into this in detail it is necessary to mention that Flying Officer Glazer has fitted to certain leading ships an IFF set similar to our auxiliary set and thus enabled the Naval formations to transmit an indication which when picked up by our ASV sets acts in a manner similar to an ASV homing beacon.

Co-operation with Naval Forces so equipped is in my opinion an idea of great possibilities but one which, due to its infancy has not yet shown great results.[1]

The policy adopted is for the leading ship, fitted with a 'Rooster' to work with an ASV Wellington so that the aircraft can, by a series of signals, lead the Naval Formation into the desired action.

The aircraft sets out to locate both the enemy (usually a convoy) and our own forces and consequently bring the two together whilst maintaining as great a degree of W/T silence as possible.

This is achieved by passing reports by visual signalling using the aircraft's downward recognition light.

To assist with this signalling a Fleet Air Arm Observer is carried as an extra member of the crew. He also assists with the sending of W/T reports and generally acts as Naval Liaison Officer.

This scheme has worked successfully on one occasion but has failed on two others due to the 'Rooster' on board not being received by the aircraft co-operating.

[1] Good results followed, almost immediately, with Naval Force K.

The 'Rooster' is at the moment a locally-manufactured installation made up out of the limited spare equipment available to Flying Officer Glazer and this fact may account for it's present state of unreliability. It would seem that, given a reliable installation and the skilled personnel to service it, the possibilities of the idea are really great and I feel sure that air to sea co-operation of this nature can help considerably in sweeping enemy shipping from the Mediterranean. I suggest that it could also be used with great effect in the Far East and in any other theatre of war where the essential problem is one of destroying enemy shipping.

Certain limitations are imposed on these operations (and others) during the non-moon period when the darkness makes the identification of ships an impossibility. On such nights the aircraft have come down to as low as 500 feet over the centre of the convoy and not been able to see anything further than a few specks of wash. Nor is one able to get a picture of the whole force, their formation, or numbers. The most reliable guide to identification is obtained from the screen of the ASV and at the best we can only report, 'approximately 8 unidentified vessels'.

Provided that the ships are moving at sufficient speed so as to leave behind a definite wake the course of the unknown ships can be determined to within 10 – 15 degrees but it is difficult to get directly over any particular ship and on occasions the aircraft has had to make as many as 5 runs towards the ASV indication before the necessary streak of wash has been seen.

During moon periods there is little difficulty in determining the composition and course of the ships although the estimation of tonnage and speed can only be very approximate.

2. **Co-operation with Swordfish aircraft of 830 Squadron**
Swordfish aircraft are fitted to carry either a torpedo or an ASV set plus a number of flares.

Their method of night attack is as follows:

Acting upon a daylight sighting report an ASV Swordfish leads a striking force of Torpedo-carrying planes to the enemy and further assists the attacking aircraft by dropping flares if required to do so.

The limitation which handicaps this very successful method of attack is the poor range of the Swordfish.

The enemy are well aware of this and in consequence pass their ships as far away as possible from the Swordfish radius of action, so that if the Swordfish are able to attack at all it can only be done with a small safety margin of petrol. The ASV Swordfish is not able therefore to spend any time searching the probable area of the enemy.

To reduce this period of searching an ASV Wellington is despatched in advance to search for the enemy. Upon sighting a W/T report is sent out and the aircraft's 'Rooster' is switched on.

Acting on this report the Swordfish aircraft, led by an ASV machine, take-off and are homed onto the convoy by receiving the Wellington's 'Rooster.' It being arranged that the Wellington remains within 5 miles of the ships when located.

This method of attack has been most successful and on every occasion when the Wellington has located the target the Swordfish have delivered a successful attack except on one occasion when the leader's ASV is believed to have broken down and the whole force was lost.[2]

The Wellington's Rooster has been consistently received at an average distance of 50 miles.

This I regard as an argument which supports the contention that a built-in 'Rooster' can be regarded as reliable as, apart from the failures of the 'Roosters' fitted to Naval Vessels, the distance at which it was picked up does not average more than 40 miles.

3. Co-operating with Albacores of 828 Squadron

When the Albacores can be fitted with ASV it seems certain that co-operation with this type of aircraft will produce similar results as co-operation with Swordfish.

At the present time however Albacores are not fitted with any form of ASV and co-operation with them is a more difficult operation and a similar one to our co-operation with Wellington aircraft detailed below; the only essential

---

[2] An explanation, from Lt Cmdr Osborn, for the loss of these aircraft is given in Chapter 3.

difference being that the Albacore carries a torpedo as against the bomb load carried by Wellingtons.

4. Co-operating with Bombers of Wellingtons from No 38, 104 and 40 Squadrons.

Wellingtons (like Albacores) are not able to locate convoys at night by ordinary means.

The procedure therefore is for our Wellington aircraft fitted with ASV to set out in advance with the object of locating the convoy. A W/T sighting report is then sent out and in reply Base inform the ASV aircraft of the ETA (Estimated Time of Arrival) of each attacking wave.

At an agreed time prior to the ETA the ASV Wellington commences to drop flares at regular intervals for the purpose of homing the attacking bombers.

The attacking aircraft signify their arrival by a pre-arranged signal and complete the attack using their own flares for any illumination required.

The results of these attacks have not been very successful. This is due to the fact that the Wellington is not a suitable aircraft for low level attacks on ships and it is a type of attack for which the crews have had no experience. Past experience has shown that the most successful method of attack against shipping is one delivered from mast height.

Perhaps an even more important consideration which limits the effectiveness of any attack brought about by this method of homing is that the flares dropped by the ASV aircraft (for homing purposes) give warning to the enemy of air attack and enable him to lay a smokescreen, an operation which he performs very cleverly and can sustain for considerable periods.

This smokescreen makes bomb aiming very difficult and completely 'blinds' Albacores attacking with torpedoes from sea level height.

To repeat once again –

Flares dropped just prior to a Swordfish attack serve a sole function of illuminating the target and the attack is delivered before the enemy can take effective counter measures.

Flares dropped by ASV Wellington for a Wellington or Albacore attack serve a dual function. Firstly of 'homing' the attacking force to the target and secondly of supplying a degree of illumination. This gives the enemy plenty of time to lay down his cover of smoke and to take up the most suitable defensive formation against the air attack which he knows is to follow.

5. Bombing attacks by ASV Wellingtons

An experiment was tried of using ASV Wellingtons for carrying out bombing attacks against enemy shipping at night.

The plan was for the aircraft to locate it's target by ASV reduce height and 'home' down to shortest possible range (about 1 mile) depending upon the state of the sea, to continue on this course and to deliver a surprise low level attack using visual means for the final sighting.

It was intended to use this method of attack on moonlight nights only it being considered too difficult to locate the ship otherwise. This method of attack has been found to be moderately successful but it requires a degree of skill to avoid hitting the ship and involves a risk which, with our limited number of aircraft, might easily jeopardise other more fruitful operations.

This idea I am convinced has great possibilities and with a greater number of aircraft available, is one which I think should be explored further. The Wellington is not a suitable aircraft for this type of attack being as it is too large for easy manoeuvrability and having a definite delay in the effectiveness of it's controls – particularly aileron controls.

Bearing in mind the factors which limit (4) and (5) above it would seem to me that the answer to solve these problems would be to use a fast medium bomber fitted with an ordinary ASV set, or even a 'skeleton' ASV set capable of receiving nothing apart from an ASV beacon as transmitted by an IFF 'Rooster'. The Hudson seems the obvious immediate choice or an ASV Beaufort or perhaps one of the American aircraft of the Boston, Baltimore type could be adapted for this purpose.

An aircraft of this kind should be able to 'home' onto anything found and should be capable of delivering a swift and effective attack.

I think too that the scheme could be worked on dark nights as well as on moonlight ones, using, if necessary, flare dropping procedures as practised by Swordfish of 830 Squadron.

6. Night Shadowing of Enemy Convoys

This is a comparatively simple operation but one which supplies useful information for a dawn strike.

It has not been used much by the Special Duties Flight as on these occasions when convoys have been found at night either the ships or aircraft operating in conjunction with ASV Wellingtons have been able to take immediate action without waiting for the dawn.

7. Sweeps along the enemy's known shipping routes

This is an operation not normally necessary in this area as the daylight reconnaissances are able to give information regarding the whereabouts of most shipping in the area.

There have been occasions however when the enemy's shipping position has been uncertain and on these occasions ASV Wellingtons have carried out more or less 'blind' sweeps.

The enemy ships remain as close as possible to the coast lines of Italy or Greece, and this fact handicaps the ASV aircraft as the ASV set is constantly recording land echoes.

The great number of Islands encountered constitute an even greater difficulty and the 'back echo' occurring up to 10 miles makes the position even more complicated.

The elimination of this back echo by the fitting of more effective reflector plates would considerably ease all operations carried out in the vicinity of island or coastline.

8. Possibility that the aircraft may be employed against enemy submarines should they constitute a menace in the area

No operations have yet been carried out against enemy submarines but it is presumed that the standard methods of attack as laid down by Coastal Command and as carried out by ASV aircraft of 221 Squadron would be carried out.

The chances of finding the submarines by use of ASV has always been slight in daylight and extremely unlikely at night due to the small indication which submarines are capable of transmitting onto an ASV receiver.

To attack with depth charges dropped from a low altitude is another difficult operation at night.

It seems likely therefore that unless the menace from submarines becomes really great our very small number of aircraft will not be employed on this work – certainly not in preference to our co-operation work with the Royal Navy and Fleet Air Arm.

The finding of a submarine in this area should be slightly easier than it was over the Atlantic due to the calmer state of the sea and the absence of the Atlantic rollers which gave indications of a size comparable with that given by submarines.

9. The proposed scheme for working in co-operation with our own Submarines

This is I suggest, impracticable unless the submarines are fitted with an efficient 'Rooster'.

As stated above to locate a submarine is extremely problematical especially when flying through bad weather.

In addition to which it seems by reports that the submarines in this area could hardly be doing better work and to risk any ship by showing vertical lights, as suggested, appears to be a risk which I doubt would be justified by the results in increased enemy sinking.

When the operation of 'Roosters' fitted to the destroyers and Cruisers has reached a state of reliability and efficiency and when the air to sea co-operation has reached an advanced stage, then, I suggest, is the time for our submarines to be included in the scheme.

The greater size of the cruisers and destroyers and their greater speed both supply reasons for assuming that air co-operation with these units could be easier than air co-operation with our own submarines as proposed.

As final remarks I should like to comment upon the state of serviceability of our ASV sets and how it compares with that experienced with 221 Squadron operating over the Atlantic on tasks of a different nature.

When we first commenced operating in October the air was warm and dry and the weather consistently good (in comparison with Atlantic weather) and results were the best that we had experienced.

Malta was picked up at maximum range (80 miles) and convoys (usually a total of about 5 vessels) up to 35 miles.

Since then however, in spite of excellent servicing from our radio mechanics the efficiency has deteriorated and there have been several instances of partial or temporary failures in the air.

This has been put down to several causes the most likely of which I consider to be:

1. Violent alterations in the engine speed necessitated by the desire of aircraft to approach their contacts on a glide so as to remain unheard. Also due to the violent avoiding action taken upon being fired at by the considerable light anti-aircraft fire of the Italian convoys.

2. The fact that our aircraft are now fitted with two long range tanks and have been operating for as long as 13 hours with the apparatus consistently switched on.

3. The appalling weather in which the aircraft have recently been operating and the remarkably damp atmosphere consistent with this time of year.

On almost all of our recent operations the aircraft have had to fly through a series of electrical storms of an intensity never experienced over the Atlantic. These storms are accompanied by violent showers.

Before finally closing I would also like to take this opportunity of expressing my appreciation of the wonderful keenness and team spirit of our entire personnel.

The aircraft have had to operate through really bad weather and the aircrew personnel have shown remarkable courage and devotion to duty by remaining on the job to the limit of their endurance so that trips over 10 hours are a common occurrence.

To single out any individual crew members or ground personnel would be to belittle the others for one and all they have been striving desperately hard to achieve the jobs given to us to do.

I remain Sirs,

Your obedient Servant.

(SGD)A SPOONER. Flt Lt 23/12/41

The foregoing report which the author submitted to the AOC Malta, Air Vice Marshal H P Lloyd, at the end of 1941 (and in all probability was typed by Nellie Galea of Chapter 9), is evidence of the manner by which junior officers, or even NCOs, could get their ideas direct to the very top. Hugh Pughe Lloyd was always willing to listen to anyone who had ideas about how the Air Force in Malta, and this included operational control over the Fleet Air Arm units stationed there, could prevent supplies reaching the enemy in North Africa. His mission was to help to cut General Rommel's supply lines.

It is also an indication of how closely the RAF, FAA and RN worked together in Malta and did so without too much regard for either ranks or established procedures. The co-operation started right at the top with Vice Admiral Ford, Major General Beak, the Army GOC and the holder of the VC and AVM Lloyd all good friends and willing helpers. Later Field Marshal Lord Gort, another holder of the VC, joined this efficient band of Service leaders when he became the Governor of Malta.

The report, which was recently unearthed for me from the Public Records Office, and which I had forgotten about for nearly 50 years, must have been labelled 'SECRET' as the then secret initials 'ASV' are mentioned therein.

THE GEORGE CROSS ISLAND ASSOCIATION

This association was founded in 1987 with Army, Navy, Air Force, Merchant Navy, nurses and Civilian Defence Services equally included. There is a large Maltese Branch which typifies the manner in which the British, Allied and Maltese people stood shoulder to shoulder against the common Axis enemy.

Among it's aims are: the continued friendship between the British and Maltese peoples; the determination to keep alive the unbreakable Malta spirit which King George VI honoured with the unique award of the George Cross: a medium by which whose who survived could get in touch with old comrades, and a determination to see that those who fell would for ever be remembered by the great Siege Bell memorial which HM the Queen unveiled in Valletta on 29th May 1992.

The Association has been prominent in two events: in supporting the aforementioned monument (Memorial) and in suggesting that a Malta Medal be awarded to each individual who contributed to overcoming Malta's enormous supply and defence difficulties. Thanks to the generosity of the Malta Government - the Malta George Cross Fiftieth Anniversary medal - was struck in April 1992 for presentation to all eligible personnel. It is regarded as a truly just reward for those who survived the dangerous convoys, the blitz and the siege.

To complement the Siege Bell in Malta, 2005 saw a memorial of Malta stone placed by the association in Tower Place, London that was dedicated in the presence of their Patron HRH The Duke of Edinburgh and the President of Malta HE Edward Fenech Adami. A fitting venue for an annual remembrance service in the UK.

More details of the association are available from their website www.georgecrossisland.org.uk or through Crécy Publishing telephone 0044 161 499 0024.

BIBLIOGRAPHY

Malta – Blitzed but not Beaten, Philip Vella,Progress Press Valletta.

Malta – The Hurricane Years, Shores, Cull & Malizia, Grub Street.

Malta – The Spitfire Year, Shores, Cull & Malizia, Grub Street.

Faith Hope & Charity, Kenneth Poolman, Kimber.

Night Strike from Malta, Kenneth Poolman, Janes.

The Right of the Line, John Terraine, Hodder & Stoughton.

One Man's Window Denis Barnham, Kimber.

The Shiphunters, R E Gillman, John Murray.

Climbing Turns, Pat Foss, Linden Hall.

The Ship – Busters, Ralph Barker, Chatto & Windus.

War in a Stringbag, Charles Lamb, Cassell.

Malta – The Thorn in Rommel's Side, Laddie Lucas, Stanley Paul.

The Air Battle of Malta, Lord James Douglas, Hamilton.